BUILD YOUR
DREAM NETWORK

BUILD YOUR DREAM NETWORK

Forging Powerful Relationships in a Hyper-Connected World

J. KELLY HOEY

A TarcherPerigee Book

tarcherperigee

An imprint of Penguin Random House LLC
375 Hudson Street
New York, New York 10014

Illustrations by Gena Cuba

Most TarcherPerigee books are available at special quantity discounts
for bulk purchase for sales promotions, premiums, fund-raising,
and educational needs. Special books or book excerpts also can be
created to fit specific needs. For details, write:
SpecialMarkets@penguinrandomhouse.com.

ISBN 9780143111481

Printed in the United States of America
3   5   7   9   10   8   6   4   2

Book design by Katy Riegel

For the world's greatest nephews plus

Luciana, Phoebe,

and Monty

Contents

A Networked Career

"Do you recognize anyone here?"

I smiled and whispered in my friend Janet's ear, "Yup. That's Ivanka Trump standing right behind you. And Tory Burch just walked in the door."

We stood in an elegant, full-floor duplex apartment on Park Avenue, where seventy-five carefully selected guests were gathered for a private reception and dinner with activist Malala Yousafzai. The guest list included Trumps, Kennedys, and Tisches. It was not a crowd I'd ever imagined mingling with when I first began my career in the beige Bay Street offices of the corporate law firm Miller Thomson.

Back then, at age twenty-three, I had no idea what I really wanted to be. Law was not some well-thought-out career plan; it just seemed a safe bet. Looking back, I think of that initial career as fulfilling more of an expectation—much like the predictable forward motion of a conveyer belt—than a proactive choice. And, really, what else do you do with an undergraduate degree in political science and economics? Back in 1988 you packed your poli-sci degree along with your big hair and mom jeans and headed off to law school.

Pursuing a passion project, starting a business, working remotely, or having several careers at once—these ideas were inconceivable. Back then they meant you either couldn't hold down a job, were unemployable, or simply lacked focus. Sharing was not a source of income, and working from home was not a real job.

Confined by the vision of my immediate connections and the economic times, the best career plan I had imagined was being rewarded with lock-step promotions up the corporate ladder. In other words, I had drunk the "work hard and get rewarded and promoted" corporate-for-life Kool-Aid.

And that exactly described the pretty humdrum treadmill of my career until 2002, when I took steps to actively change direction.

How? Looking back, the common thread to my professional life (which has zigged and zagged from suits in office towers to coworking spaces to coffee shops to private airplanes, VIP rooms, and speaker podiums) has been networks and an active focus on creating powerful connections.

If you're reading this and dreading another book about how to work a room or hand out business cards while munching on chicken satay, you can relax—randomly schmoozing is not what I am talking about here. I hate walking into rooms filled with strangers. And I actively avoid hors d'oeuvres served on a stick.

Haphazardly circling rooms filled with strangers is old school and counterproductive. I'm not in sales, nor am I an extrovert (actually I'm an ambivert, squarely situated between introverts and extroverts),[1] so I avoid what I call "random acts of networking." If I could find a better word to use than "networking" I would, but for now my goal is to change what you think that activity is and, more important, how you go about doing it.

Networking is a way to go about solving a problem.

My aha! moment first came in 2002, when I was exhausted from working by the billable hour and needed a new career focus for my legal education and eleven years of transactional experience. As a first step, I spent eighteen months actively cultivating a legal-management-focused network in order to transition out of the practice of law and into law firm management.

I broke free; I reengaged with my career; I networked more. In 2009 I became a member of 85 Broads, a global business network for women, and nine months later ended up its first president. I signed up for an angel-investment boot camp in 2012, and with that experience in my wallet, I transformed my career opportunities again as I began angel investing in emerging tech. My investments diversified along with my networks. My contact base and dinner invites tripled. My confidence in my career choices and investments skyrocketed. Later I joined the cofounders of the startup accelerator Women Innovate Mobile. They'd been looking for a third partner, and every single networking outreach effort they made led them to me. When you know people, and those people know what you do, success knows how to find you.

By setting specific goals first—key to initiating any networking process—I've networked and successfully connected online, in person, at receptions and on committees, via e-mail and, yes, occasionally over a caffeinated beverage. Today, not some but *all* my opportunities arise from and because of the strength of my network and the way I go about connecting.

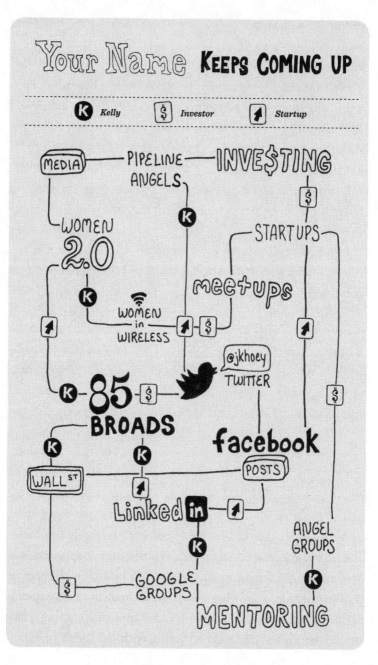

And this includes opportunities for others. I am constantly asked for introductions or advice.

The process of purposefully making connections and strategically building and then activating networks of personal relationships has fueled each phase of my evolving career, and I strongly suspect it will define my opportunities to come. And my timing in evolving these skills has collided perfectly with dynamic and powerful shifts in the way we work, spend money, and interact.

Access Is the New Economy

Whatever you call the dynamics of the disruptive and transformational economic order we are in—the "access," "peer-driven," "democratized," "sharing," or "collaborative" economy (the list of names for it goes on)—the result is the same: it has fundamentally changed how we communicate, catch a ride to work, deliver a package, learn a new skill, monetize a hobby, connect with a colleague in the office, find a job, locate expertise, and plan a holiday. For a growing number of people, gone are the days of the regular commute to the same office building: 34 percent of those employed in the United States are now freelancers, and that number is predicted to jump to 40 percent by 2020![2] Almost 3 percent of Americans work remotely at least part of the time. Online peer-driven platforms now book more guest rooms than established old-economic-model hotel chains. The part of the new economy that prioritizes on-demand access over ownership is expected to reach $335 billion in revenue[3] in the next decade, a growing economic movement that is upending how, when, and on what terms we approach earning a living, starting a business, and engaging with colleagues.

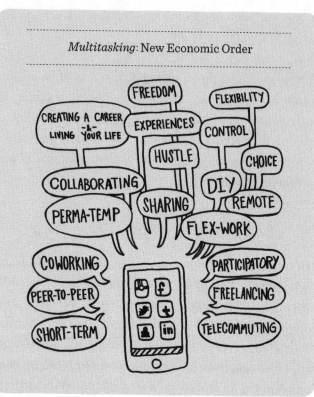

Or is it?

Weirdly, the shift to a peer-to-peer networked economy—away from buying cars, designer gowns, and vacation packages and toward seeking mobility, experiences, and convenience—simply highlights the increased importance of human capital and personal connections. That capital comes in the form of trusted relationships: mentors, advisors, sponsors, boards of directors, references, referrals. Same as it always has!

This is the human capital in your network—people who can and will use their resources (including money, reputation, and experience) to:

- ❏ Spread word of mouth
- ❏ Make recommendations and open doors for you
- ❏ Send work your way
- ❏ Offer you a job
- ❏ Make introductions
- ❏ Vouch for your credentials
- ❏ Cheer you on
- ❏ Write you a check
- ❏ Right a social networking wrong
- ❏ Ignite a campaign
- ❏ Start a grassroots effort
- ❏ Close a funding gap
- ❏ Create opportunities
- ❏ Set a future direction
- ❏ And reboot your efforts

The ability to tap into and leverage these kinds of connections matters more than ever as trust becomes the foundation of new peer-driven platforms. But hasn't it always been the foundation for professional or business success? People open doors, write checks, and extend opportunities—always have. Need something? Turn to your immediate, trusted network of friends for recommendations. The big difference now is that we turn instinctively to those close, trusted relationships with a click, using technology as the intermediary for our most important (and sometimes intimate) asks.

When I think about the key turning points in my career, I see that although each occurred during an economic downturn, I was able to harness connections and navigate my way to new opportunities. To take advantage of this new economy you have to evolve how you think about connecting to your network, just as you have reimagined your relationships with cars, homes, and other property over the years. The über-economic transformation we're experiencing hasn't changed the rules; it's simply revealed what the real career-success rules have always been.

In networking, those career-success rules are based on principles of generosity and trust. This is old wisdom and still holds true; we simply have many more engagement tools to work with now. Today a Facebook update stands alongside the printed birthday card as a way to stay in touch. It may seem strange, but tweets, pins, and likes are acts of generosity in the new networking era. Helping someone else's blog post reach a wider audience is a great way to build rapport and to get their attention.

For many of us, new networking options multiply daily (maybe a new instant-messaging app or Instagram integration or affinity group at the office), so it's key not to get too distracted by these shiny new technology options and lose sight of the intended purpose of our networking efforts.

Seem overwhelming? It isn't really. In this book I will provide you with a uniquely goal-focused networking process, not simply an admonishment to use such and such tools in your networking efforts. And, obviously, for different goals some communication tools will be more effective than others.

New networking necessitates carefully cultivating relationships made with the help of close, trusted contacts, then casting a wider net beyond that immediate circle of trust. It is the intentional pursuit of a goal, one networking *act* achieved by multiple, focused networking *actions*.

New networking means getting to know people online to secure the meeting offline. Take Jennifer as an example. Jennifer is the founder of a technology platform that connects up-and-coming brands with social influencers. She has relocated her startup to New York City in order to meet people at major fashion brands and other potential customers. Her challenge is to quickly build trust in the social networking world so these individuals will agree to meet with her. Social influencers are online, so Jennifer has to build rapport on their turf (Instagram, Snapchat, Twitter, Periscope) if she has the slightest hope of securing an in-person meeting. The authenticity and believability of her networking approach has to align with the core offering of her startup. If she doesn't display the same transparent networking tactics as the influencers she's looking to attract to her platform, her credibility with both influencers and brands is over!

The new networking tactics for Jennifer, before she even asks to meet for coffee, are to:

- Not only follow these targets on social media, but retweet, like, repost, and pin their content
- Subscribe to their newsletters, blogs, YouTube channels, and podcasts (and then share insights with her network)
- Join their meetup groups
- Participate in the live video-streaming sessions they conduct (plus promote and live-tweet them)

Those who can cut through the noise of our hyperconnected world of likes, favorites, friends, and followers to harness the true value of a network are not only surviving in the new "access" economy but also seamlessly moving between online and offline networking worlds, and thriving in the connections process.

New networking tactics are not just for individuals: to be successful, corporations need to embrace social platforms, transform closed office environments into collaborative work spaces, and examine the networks they'll need to nurture to conduct business in the years to come. The Cleveland Clinic is a leading example of an organization actively anticipating the future possibilities of its business needs. It has forged partnerships with NASA[4] (who better than NASA to advise on teamwork and innovative "space-age" materials) as well as with Cox Communications.[5] Cox provides entertainment, high-speed Internet, home security, and phone service to approximately a third of US households. As medical advice and records increasingly move to mobile platforms (and out of the doctor's office to the patient's home), the Cleveland Clinic understands it needs critical insights into the digital habits of its patients.

Here are more examples of corporations tracking and embracing the new networking order in everything from the way they approach new business opportunities to the C-suite positions they hire:

- In early 2016, GM entered into an alliance with the ride-hailing startup Lyft[6] to allow would-be drivers to rent GM cars in order to work for Lyft. GM sees the future of auto use—on-demand, mobile, and urban—shifting more rapidly in the next five years than it has in the past fifty. Not to miss out on this opportunity, it has invested $500 million to deeply integrate and innovate with Lyft.

- The Agile Workplace (a research partnership between Gartner Inc., MIT, and twenty-two industry sponsors)[7] has concluded that the most successful organizations are also the most agile. Agile organizations are those that can form work teams quickly in order to connect to new opportunities or to address changes in the business environment.

- IBM recommended its employees get on the intranet back in 1997![8] Embracing social tools (along with a people-centric approach to social media) has been a key factor in IBM's transformation. Big Blue has a four-hundred-thousand-plus-strong internal social network, enabling employees to locate and tap into a massive network of expertise to solve client problems (as well as to crowdsource solutions to their own).

- Steelcase, a global leader in office furniture, has been watching the "trend to bench"—the long workbench-style table, that is.[9] Yes, the workbench is making a comeback as employees escape from the traditional office environment's cubicle. The workbench solves many of the workplace challenges that result from a mobile, social, and transient workforce (consider the setup of your local Starbucks or coworking space, locations that typically make use of long, communal tables). Let's face it, office workspaces today have to adapt easily as business needs rapidly shift and evolve in the new economy. The office environment also needs to encourage networking. As Steelcase notes, "The fast-growing number of mobile workers who want to 'see and be seen' during the times they come into the office, thereby quickly connecting and catching up with coworkers," is fueling the bench trend. Who could have predicted that face time at the office would be more important than ever before?

- In a rapidly evolving economic order, work environments that invite casual collaboration (such as informal meeting spaces) are increasingly important. At the offices of business management consultant Humantech, the workplace is now designed to support collegial relationships. Eighty percent of its workspaces are unassigned and informal collaboration spaces, strategically located throughout the office. Movement in the workplace is encouraged—to create more "water-cooler" moments.[10]

- Some researchers have suggested that the time has come for organizations to hire chief collaboration officers— because efficient sharing of informational, social, and personal resources between employees and strong internal networks are needed to solve many of the most pressing business challenges organizations are facing today.[11]

Skills Alone Won't Make You a Success

These truths might make you either uncomfortable or really excited:

- Everyone is an expert
- College degrees can be bypassed
- Anyone can start a company—anywhere
- Meritocracy is BS

Back in 1988 scores, rankings, percentiles, and grades were all you needed to get that first, coveted "foot on the corporate ladder" job. What you knew, as delineated by those numbers, and where you earned your degree, really mattered back then.

But today a degree doesn't automatically make you marketable. No, the new question is not what you know but *Who knows what you know?*

Who knows that you do what you do better than anyone

else? Who has heard your unique point of view? Who knows what product you're developing or passion project you're pursuing?

Your skills and expertise need an audience. We live in an era of abundance, and good ideas are a dime a dozen. It's the ideas without a network that don't launch, scale, or sell.

Great ideas, and great opportunities, have networks behind them. Active networks of champions, fans, enthusiasts, early adopters, influencers—people invested in the success of the ideas' creators. New ideas don't come to life at arm's distance; they emerge from an embrace.

Starting up or Starting Over (Again): Start with Your Network

It's become obvious to me that professional hurdles (whether career transitions, crowdfunding projects, or financing for new ventures) should be approached as networking challenges. And therefore a unique network will form the solution for each.

Let's assume you're reading this book because you're thinking about launching a new career or venture. Your first reaction may be to look into a "careers you may be interested in" posting you've seen next to your LinkedIn profile, or you could resort to e-mailing absolutely everyone you know and telling them you're thinking about changing careers or launching a business. Both tactics miss the mark (unless you enjoy agonizing over the lack of interesting offers you're receiving).

The better plan is to:

A. Know what you want
B. Know who to ask for help in getting what you want
C. Know how to ask for that help

The process requires strategic planning—and the reality is that to scale a successful venture requires work and a process. Tapping into the right network of people is key to the successful execution of each and every one of your career or professional or business plans, but you have to be prepared to put in the work.

Yes, it is called net*working* for a reason.

How to Use This Book

- Grab a pen and write in this book.
- Fold the page corners.
- Highlight passages.
- Crack the spine.
- Add your own ideas.

This book is intended to be your reference and guide to networking in this new economic order. Some information contained between these covers may be very familiar to you or may be a reminder of a networking route or process you were advised to take before—and perhaps ignored. Use this book to make your own networking to-do lists and to set your goals on the path to networked success.

And, yes, while we live in a selfie-infused, hyperactive (as well as -connected) world, this book is not just about how I've networked *my* way from practicing law to a dinner with Malala. I've leaned on a lot of people I know who have achieved success by setting clear goals then tapping into their networks, and

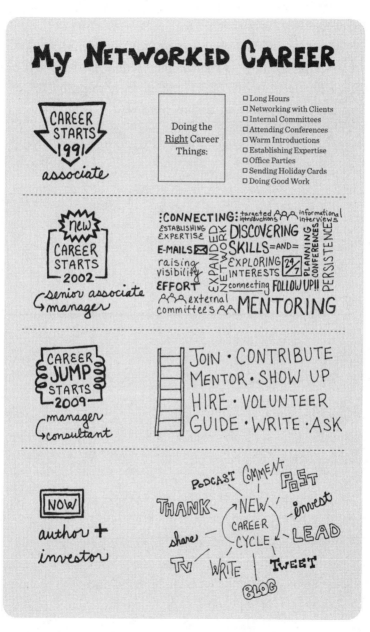

their stories are in here too. So it's not just network as I say; it's network as my network does too!

Whatever you do with this book, don't simply read it. Take what you're learning and put it into action. Daily. You'll be amazed as exciting new opportunities, friendships, invites, offers, and thank-yous start to come your way.

1

Build Your Network

NETWORKING NEEDS A rebranding.

When I asked my friend Jonathan Beninson what he thinks when he hears the word "networking," his rapid-fire response was "Those moments when you exchange business cards with someone and figure out how you can benefit from them."

Ouch! A painful but definitely not atypical reaction to hearing the word "networking"—and an honest account of what we generally think networking is.

Jonathan is the chief strategy officer at House of Genius, a growing global community of entrepreneurs and innovative thinkers, so he knows a thing or two about forging strong relationships. Like Jonathan, I really do wish there was another word for the activities we undertake to connect and strengthen our relationships with other people, but this is the one we seem to be stuck with.

Merriam-Webster defines "networking" as "the exchange of information or services among individuals, groups, or institutions; *specifically*: the cultivation of productive relationships for employment or business." Not a motivating definition in alignment with the new economic dynamic and hyperconnected world we live in (and the definition sounds a lot like the activity Jonathan abhors).

I look to the definition of "net" for inspiration instead—"an openwork fabric made of threads or cords that are woven or knotted together at regular intervals"—because for me networking is an ongoing process of establishing and strengthening relationships. It is not confined to a single activity such as e-mail introductions or cocktail receptions in the lobby of a corporation's headquarters. And it is so much more than simply handing over a business card. It is continually connecting to build stronger connections (or to expand the strength of an existing network). It is weaving online and offline interactions into an integrated networking whole. As I see it, regular intervals of networking now include the person you choose to sit next to in a coworking space or the Twitter follower's daily insight you eagerly seek out, or perhaps it is the good old birthday greeting, be it a text, Facebook post, or emoji.

Whatever we call the activity, here's why I'm so passionate about it: networking has made my every career jump possible, and it can do the same for you.

My career in New York—from work assignments to opportunities to join committees or not-for-profit boards to job offers—can be traced back to my network. There's the network I brought with me from Toronto in 1998, when I arrived in New York City. My contact list was six people deep back then. It was a completely different story in 2009 when I "jumped" from the safety of a paycheck to the possibility of making a living on the basis of my community-building expertise. In 2010 I jumped again, from the comfort of a single innovative client (85 Broads) to a new, expanded client base of established blue-chip companies along with new-economy innovators, investors, and technology entrepreneurs. Pocketing that experience (and a new diverse group of business connections), in 2011 I jumped into angel investing and later that year my network bubbled up the visionary idea of cofounding a startup accelerator.

I say this because I've lived it: mentors, advisors, role models, and diverse networks provide the support for possibilities and encourage us to jump beyond our biggest hesitations.

Connections Fuel a Career

I didn't set out to be a "networker" or "connector"—titles others anointed me with, people who have observed the unfolding of my career and the ways I have guided others to achieve their goals. I have come to understand the value of my approach to networking, with the benefit of experience and a whole lot of hindsight. Each career move and opportunity has come about as the result of a connection—that is, as the result of a real, human, and personal relationship, versus random acts of strangers or help-wanted ads or algorithms.

Here's my career-momentum formula →

The people in my network opened doors at critical junctures in my career because I'd already established relationships with them, so they knew what I was capable of achieving. Having a network altered not only my career path but

also my perspective on what I could be and, more important, the power I had to do the same for someone else.

Expertise and a goal are just your starting point. Networks are crucial because gaining access changes your outcome.

Goals Need a Network Plus Action

Becoming a law-firm partner had lost its allure for me by 2001. With no interest in grabbing that shiny brass ring, I sat down to focus on plan B. I assessed my work environment and interactions with colleagues. I thought about the seventy-plus-hour workweeks I regularly put in. From my back-of-the-envelope career assessment, I quickly realized that I wanted to stay in the legal profession and needed to find a role helping other attorneys succeed (mentoring junior associates had provided me with great career satisfaction).

Prior to 2002, I had a business network of lawyers and investment bankers. Get the pulse of Wall Street? No problem; my network could easily provide those insights. It was when I longed to take my career beyond purchase and sale agreements that I realized the vast limitations of my network. So in the spring of 2002, my career plan B became the following:

- Build a brand-new network of connections with people on the management side of the legal profession whose functions primarily focused on attorney training and career development, and
- Network my butt off with these new connections and their industry peers from other cities so they would know me, understand my capabilities, and keep me top-of-mind when positions opened up.

This was the plan I focused on until 2004, when I landed *the* dream position at White & Case LLP. I won't lie: there were a couple of near misses along the way and, yes, a few diversions caused by meetings with recruiters as a result of job postings I had read (a "don't leave any rock unturned" mentality crept into my anxious job-seeking brain at times). But in the end, someone who knew me and understood my abilities because we regularly stayed in touch called to ask me to interview for a new role at the global law firm. I was the only candidate the firm interviewed. I got the call and the job because I'd been persistent in my networking.

As I set out to build a new professional network, I understood that I was doing so not only to land a new job; I was building a network to do my new dream job. What a waste it would have been to fail to continue the connections I'd made with all those professional peers simply because I'd landed the job! Having a trusted network of industry peers who had experience in the role I was just stepping into made it much easier to get over the management learning curve (not to mention the benefit of having a sounding board on which to test my ideas).

Passion, talent, and hard work are not the only ingredients for success. Whether it is changing careers or changing the world, an idea without a network will probably never become reality. And the network of contacts you need in order to break through is often the network that initially fuels your career momentum. Though called upon less frequently now, my former colleagues in Toronto continue to be vital components of my network.

Networks determine which ideas become breakthrough innovations—and who gets introductions, offers, and all the other career and life perks that come with knowing someone in the know. Continually engaging and expanding my network is no longer my plan B; it is a professional priority. It is plan A.

Your next goal or career ambition—whether it's a promotion, landing a coveted internship, launching your own company, securing a board seat, crowdfunding a project, or appearing on CNBC's *Power Pitch*—needs a game plan! Look at your network. Where are the missing links and where are the overlooked or missed connections?

What do you need to start doing today to create better connections?

What Networking Really Is

Not only do I hate walking into rooms filled with strangers, but I am deeply suspicious of anyone who says they really enjoy it. If you really, I mean *really*, enjoy stepping into a room where you do not know a soul, then you're likely a fine-tuned, heat-seeking sales machine and I'd rather navigate the scent-spritzing gauntlet of the perfume department at Saks than be cornered by you at a networking event.

Another confession: I hate "lists" that make the activity of networking sound easy (such as "five things every successful networker does on Monday morning") because if there was a definitive list of five things that we had to do to network successfully, well, we'd all be doing them, wouldn't we? We're not fools for being confused or anxious about networking as an activity; we're just human.

What I do know about networking is this:

- It is an essential and continual activity.
- You control the effort—but not the outcome.
- Networking is *everywhere*.

Successful networking requires understanding the immense power of regular daily activities to connect with someone else.

These are all networking activities:

1. Your e-mail signature line
2. The wording of your out-of-office autoresponder
3. Your voicemail message
4. Your profile on a website
5. An update posted on your LinkedIn profile (or the headline you use on LinkedIn)
6. Your headshot on a social media profile
7. Your bio as a speaker or award recipient or board appointee
8. Your invoice
9. The music that plays when a customer is on hold
10. Participating in a Twitter chat

How you present yourself in any of these "networking encounters" is as important as a VIP invitation, a solid handshake, or a slick elevator pitch.

Networking Is Still Work

Networks are my career fuel and constant work focus, because I learned how much time it takes to build a new network back in 2002. It was a tremendous eighteen-month effort to purposefully build, activate, and engage a new professional network! Don't get me wrong: there were some good networking times as I got to know my industry peers and understand the issues they faced on a daily basis in their various roles. But even as I bonded

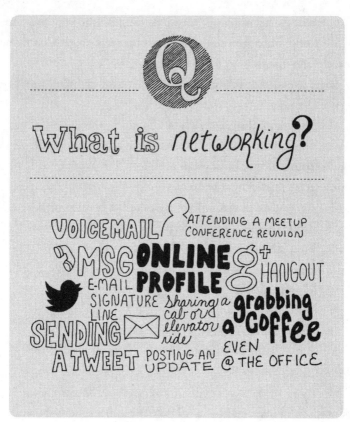

over wine and commiserated with them about how difficult attorneys can be, it was still work.

My networking was focused not simply on landing a new job (and earning a regular paycheck) but on landing a *particular* job: a role in attorney training and development at a major global law firm. To make the career transition, I set out to become an expert in the field *before* I had the title or business card. I researched the issues my peers were wrestling with every day. I took courses on training, coaching, and human-resource issues at NYU's School of Continuing and Professional Studies. I attended industry conferences and wrangled my way onto bar association committees. I kept my job search targeted and my networking efforts highly focused.

So here is another big insight from those eighteen months: networking is all about strategic curiosity.

What does that mean? It means you need to stop googling and demanding an answer every time you make an ask. We live in a hyperconnected world of instantaneous expectations. We type search terms into our web browser and hit Enter with the expectation of an immediate answer. Immediacy of results takes precedence over curiosity, inquiry, and consideration (does anyone look beyond the first page of search results?). Having access to unlimited amounts of information at the touch or swipe of a screen means we should do something more than simply react to it!

You Can't Hack Relationships

Networking is hard because it involves people.

My three Ps of networking are: People. People. People. No, it's not about the platform (or the association, organization, group, or event)! Networking is always about the people—who they are, how they engage, how they want to be reached, how they cluster—and until you truly internalize that, your networking efforts won't be effective.

If you focus on spreadsheets, formulas, and connectivity apps, you forget that you're really connecting with another person. Every transaction or connection can be justified if you only focus on tallying up columns and fail to consider the nuances of off-balance-sheet items. Dragging, flicking, and swiping may provide a better user experience in an app, but it does not establish a real human bond. When you forget the actual people behind the technology, networking becomes a transactional exercise and basic human consideration (aka generosity) flies out the window too.

Before cofounding a startup accelerator, I managed and studied numerous networking communities from corporate affinity groups to global paid-membership networks. I can promise you that every community, even within the same industry or among people with the same professional status, has a unique culture and value proposition to its members.

Why? Communities are built upon the personalities and desires of their individual members. No two chambers of commerce are the same, regardless of the similarity of their bylaws and mission statements. To say the communities on LinkedIn operate a little differently from those on Twitter would be an understatement.

You can't make strong connections by simply launching a slick conference app or rebranding a membership network. A tap or a swipe is not the foundation for trust. It's all about staying focused on people.

Expert Insight: Give Forward

Evan Nisselson is a serial entrepreneur who now invests in visual technologies via his fund, LDV Capital. He has a people-first networking philosophy, shaped by the seven years he spent in Silicon Valley when he was in his early twenties. There, in the center of global innovation, he learned—and lived—the "give forward" mentality. Evan was well versed in New York's direct "here's what I need" networking style before he relocated to Silicon Valley, so he was absolutely stunned when influential people reached out to him with offers to help without him having first asked for it. He sums up the networking ethos of Silicon Valley at the time as "everyone can benefit from some help."

This is the philosophy Evan brings to the community of more than 750 members he has built one monthly dinner at a time. The goal of the dinners is to make win-win introductions and to help people reach mutually beneficial goals. It is not networking for the sake of networking—random schmoozing is an activity Evan, even with all his global connections, does not enjoy.

Q: How do you define "community"?

Evan: "Community" for me means like-minded people getting together, having fun, and helping each other out so they can reach their goals.

Q: What do you look for in community members?

Evan: The LDV community is a monthly gathering of investors and tech entrepreneurs, so as a starting point, I seek out domain experts on the investment side (venture capitalists, angel investors, strategic investors), as well as with the innovators invited (technical as well as nontechnical founders). Gender parity is important to me. I want the guests around the table to reflect the diversity I see in the New York tech ecosystem. Finally, I want to be surrounded by thoughtful, trustworthy people who do more than simply talk. I invite people who are getting things done and who want to help others get more done. By building a community a dinner at a time, I've discovered that the community filters out the guests who "don't get it."

What I've learned from Silicon Valley is that the best communities are not reliant on one person; rather, they are strengthened by many committed members. Layering "many" on top of a giving-forward mentality is very powerful. It makes me really happy when I see the community creating opportunities for each other. Book in a Box [a book-writing and publishing company founded by the best-selling author Tucker Max] resulted from a community dinner. One dinner guest solving the problem of another dinner guest, whether it is getting a book published or finding a technology evangelist, validates coming to the table with a giving-forward approach.

Q: What's the biggest networking issue for you?

Evan: We're all human, which means we're all more or less self-focused and constantly thinking about our own immediate needs. To be successful these days, you need to not only think about what you're interested in doing (or achieving); you need to think with *and*—as in "and what is the person I'm interested in meeting with interested in?" When a connection benefits both, it is more valuable for both.

When I started the dinner community, I may have imagined I could change the attitudes of those who had not fully embraced the giving-forward approach. It doesn't work. I now focus on empowering those who do, and we have a stronger community for it.

Network to Scale

I hope you're seeing now that networking is a process with a purpose. Follow a process to connect with the right networks and, chances are, by making connections in the right way, you'll achieve your desired result.

Quick networking history quiz: has anyone heard of William Dawes?

The success of the American Revolution was the result of one man knowing which doors to knock on first to activate his entire network.[12] No, that man wasn't William Dawes. Dawes did ride out with Paul Revere on the evening of April 18, 1775, yet the history books only mention Revere.

My networking-based view on why Revere was successful: Revere understood how to activate and leverage his network quickly and effectively—and by having this strategic insight he changed the course of history (with the help of his connections, of course).

Revere got results.

Revere was a silversmith and early industrialist. Dawes was a tanner. Both men were from comparable social circles, so the imbalance in their results from undertaking the same networking task cannot be attributed to education or wealth or influence or profession or differences in social circles. It can, however, be attributed to Revere scaling his efforts by understanding which doors to knock on first, as well as knowing what he needed to ask his network to do for him.

Are you using every tool at your disposal to scale your networking efforts?

Networking to scale is about achieving your goal. In a hyperconnected world, it is also about making sure every asset you throw behind your networking efforts—from your corporate bio to your social media profiles to your e-mail signature line to the relationships you have with coworkers in your department (and across the company)—is supporting the professional objective you've set.

Back in 2008, when I was still a manager at White & Case, I switched departments to take on the challenge of invigorating the alumni program for the global law firm. This challenge was made more interesting, shall we say, by a lack of resources—my new role came with only a title. I had no staff, and zero marketing budget was allocated for the task. To accomplish anything (let alone complete daily tasks) I needed to convince a lot of my colleagues to take time away from their "real" jobs to help me. I've never been more grateful for having invested the time to get to know my colleagues in the firm and build relationships across numerous departments and offices.

Beyond lacking a staff and budget for this important initiative, I didn't have an accurate alumni list. Hundreds of professionals had left the firm over the years and were working at banks, corporations, government agencies, or competitor firms— and I had no idea who these people were.

So just how do you build an alumni program when you don't even know who the members are? One member at a time and by leveraging the power of community. I used a carefully worded outreach message tied to a role-specific social media profile. My social media profiles (LinkedIn, Facebook) got a makeover. I was now identified as the manager of alumni programs. All my social profiles reflected my laser focus: to find, connect with, and engage alumni. I was a single-interest social media user for fifteen months—networking on those platforms to rebuild the firm's alumni-engagement initiative. There was no ambiguity to what I was doing. The InMail I sent out was completely aligned with my experience on my LinkedIn profile. I posted regular updates highlighting achievements of the firm's alumni, new partner appointments, significant cases, and firm events. My networking activities were as purposeful and focused as my profile was easy to find. And I've never been more appreciative of the freemium business model (remember, I had no budget!).

I took a strategic approach to connecting and engaging with a community—and it worked (without meaningless schmoozing or analyzing endless spreadsheets of outdated information)!

To get the job done, you need networking support and to use your networking resources intelligently to scale your needs. For me, it was the strong relationships I'd established and the clarity of focus of my online networking.

Consistency Wins the Race

This is another unsexy part about networking: consistent actions produce results more often than serendipitous encounters with a dream client on an airplane. Think sit-ups: consistency is where the networking commitment hits the road to networked success.

Joe Styler at GoDaddy is exhibit A. (Joe's career-networking insights are detailed in chapter 3.) Throughout his ten-year career at GoDaddy, Joe has applied a networking formula of meeting the people he needs to learn from, following up with them to stay top-of-mind, and investing in the careers of his own team. The result for Joe is that he not only has the job he wants; he also has a powerful network within GoDaddy and across his industry.

Don't get discouraged when success doesn't happen overnight—send that follow-up e-mail to a valuable connection instead.

Expert Insight: Etiquette in the Emoji Era

How do you invite people to a dinner party?

- E-mail
- Phone call

- Facebook group
- E-vite
- Event marketing platform splash
- Text
- Written invitation posted in the mail
- In person
- One or more of these methods—it depends
- Never

Hallmark cards and custom stationery may have gone the way of the JPEG but that doesn't mean your communications or etiquette need to suffer. No one knows this better than Erin Newkirk. Erin founded Red Stamp, a technology company that makes it easy to thank, announce, wish, or simply say hi from your mobile device, desktop, or, yes, even on paper with an old-fashioned snail-mail stamp. Erin launched Red Stamp in 2005, before the onslaught of social and mobile communications. Facebook, Twitter, Snapchat, Instagram, and Pinterest may have revolutionized how many people you can message on birthdays and anniversaries; however, Erin understands that truly connecting and building strong relationships is not simply about pushing communications out on milestone events.

As I recall, Erin and I first "met" on a listserv, connecting on shared points of view. Our friendship moved off the listserv and onto e-mail (and likely Facebook as well as LinkedIn) before we finally met in person when Erin was the guest speaker at a founder's breakfast I organized during the summer of 2012.

Q: You launched, scaled, and sold a social commerce company focused on improving connections between people. What human interactions did you observe that made you stop to think there is a better or more meaningful way for connections to occur?

Erin: Red Stamp's mission always has been to be make relationships stronger—cut through the puffery of the etiquette business and get to the heart of what etiquette sets out to do: establish and maintain a set of guidelines to help people comfortably build their business and personal relationships through well-established and agreeable ground rules.

At Red Stamp, we like to say we help people celebrate and elevate the everyday in an efficient, beautiful, inexpensive way, when the mood hits them—real time, ahead of time, or spur of the moment. There truly are so many ways to say all the things you want to say these days. But one thing hasn't changed: it's the thought that counts . . . not the fact that you have stamps and engraved stationery on hand.

And while social media has its doubters and naysayers, I think it's amazing that we have the ability to be back in touch with friends from different parts of life, people who we may have thought we'd never see again postgraduation or after relocating for a job. In many ways mobile and social technology have enriched correspondence. With mobile connection, you can assure your hostess that she really was the mostest the moment you walk out her door. You can spread the pure joy of a birthday gift on Instagram with your friends and family located across the globe. One post on Facebook and you've got an impromptu porch party with friends in Minnesota celebrating the fact that it is seventy-five degrees in November.

Q: Describe how people are connecting with Red Stamp's tools. What have you observed? Was it what you expected?

Erin: Not surprisingly, thank-yous and birthdays remain the top occasions, with support, outreach, and business notes not far behind. I wanted Red Stamp to be about the everyday, and it is. It's the real-life platform for people to express feelings and connect, as they want, when they want, how they want. And, yes, a large volume of messages are sent out on Valentine's Day.

Q: What was a pivotal business networking moment for you?

Erin: Last year, I was asked to teach a class for Alt Summit on networking. Enquiring minds wanted to know . . . what was my secret sauce? The title (and opening line) of my presentation sums up my pivotal moment . . . Before this I really had not given much thought to "how" I network. My presentation was called "Relationships Are Your Secret Weapon," and the takeaway was "It pays off (big time) to be nice."

Q: Generosity is a key element of successful networking efforts. What does it mean to you in the context of Red Stamp? What guidance do you have for others on being generous in the age of omnichannel networking?

Erin: On networking and generosity, I basically have three pieces of advice:

> **It's all about gratitude.** Gratitude takes many forms, but it all starts from the heart. What works for me is to say thank you and to be thankful. It's how I end almost every conversation and oftentimes how I introduce myself or say

hello. ("Hello, my name is Erin and I am grateful to be here. Thank you for having me.") It's about thinking during every experience and every day—the bad ones and the good ones—"what am I grateful for right now?" Because there is always something to be grateful for. You learn something from everything. Gratitude can be scary. Gratitude means opening yourself up to others.

Give before you get. The smartest people I know start building relationships before they "need" them. And they do so with a clear, kind heart. Offer up help before you need or even expect a thing. Help someone you are qualified to help and find fulfillment in that.

Keep in touch. This doesn't always mean a note or a call. It could mean buying someone a cup of coffee—either in person or sending them a five-dollar Starbucks gift card along with a sweet sentiment. Sending flowers is often a day brightener. Keeping in touch could also be through gestures, like endorsing skills on LinkedIn or reposting thought provoking articles.

Q: Building community is time-consuming. How do you balance that reality against a world demanding immediate gratification?

Erin: Always realize you and your relationships are a work in progress. When someone crosses my mind, I try to let them know it in the moment with a call, text, or e-mail message rather than "saving up" my words of love and appreciation for birthdays or a winter holiday card or when I need/want something from them.

I find that the shorter, more frequent outreach facilitates comfort and authenticity.

Q: How does online networking download into the "real" world for you?

Erin: There are still real people at the start and stop of every interaction, no matter where or how it takes place. I can't help but envision the realness of the person I am chatting with in real life or online—their struggles, their accomplishments, their challenges and strengths.

Q: What are your essential (tech) business networking tools?

Erin: Red Stamp, LinkedIn, e-mail, and, yes, the Starbucks app.

A Network Alone Won't Get You to Mars

Deep networks of close friends, mentors, and advisors are needed for feedback, guidance, and advice. Then broad, expansive networks are needed to connect to opportunities and ideas that come from outside the knowledge base or expertise of your close, inner circle. Recognize that you need both types of networks and recognize that you'll use them differently.

Whether you're an entrepreneur or a job seeker, you need to throw your networking net far and wide; otherwise you risk limiting your opportunities to the boundaries of your existing networks.

Expert Insight: The Invitation Game

Sandy Cross has worked in the golf industry for close to twenty years. She's now senior director of diversity and inclusion for the

PGA of America. With experience and networking, she has evolved and expanded her role at the PGA of America from a career that started in business development to spearheading the organization's inclusion initiatives. Identifying new networks has been critical to Sandy's career advancement—from her ability to identify and develop new business opportunities to the programming she now leads to bring more women and minorities into the game.

Recall that I mentioned the importance of putting every tool at your disposal when you're networking? Sandy and I originally connected because of a blog post I wrote on how learning to play golf had helped me make important client connections early on in my legal career, and I've now had the privilege of presenting at two of Sandy's PGA events.

Q: You've described golf as a relationship business. What do you mean by that?

Sandy: The game essentially begins with an invitation. Golf is typically not a sport you take up on your own. Ask someone who plays golf how they got started in the game. Invariably someone invited them the first time they went to the course or practice range. Sure, you could get started on your own or practice or play on your own, but more often than not you are in the company of someone else. That is one of the things that make the sport so special. There are not many other sports where you can spend hours with your playing partners and carry on meaningful personal and professional conversations at the same time.

Q: Connecting professional women from different industries who share an interest in the game is one of your recent initiatives at the PGA. How did you achieve that?

Sandy: Recognizing the power of golf to build and foster connections, we launched Beyond the Green events at the PGA of America. During the week of our major championships, such as the PGA Championship and the Ryder Cup, we invite executive women, entrepreneurs, and small-business owners on-site for an up-close-and-personal look at the event. The day's activities include expert panel discussions, a keynote speaker, a behind-the-scenes tour of championship operations, and plenty of opportunities to network. Everything we do is with an eye toward fostering connections—visible name badges with company names, seating at round or communal tables, and plenty of breaks in the program for conversation. While Beyond the Green doesn't include any hands-on golf instruction, the day's activities bring the women up close to the sport and help break down the mystique and intimidation that often exists around it. By having golfers and nongolfers in attendance, the nongolfers can lean on the golfers for information about getting started in the game.

Q: Having attended Beyond the Green events, I've seen firsthand the depth of your network in the golf community. How has internal networking factored into your career success?

Sandy: I think many people view networking one-dimensionally and think only about those outside of their organization or field. So many of my external relationships in the golf and sports industry started through an internal relationship. I found my colleagues to be more than willing to extend access to their network to me, and in turn I have done the same for them. This approach makes the work environment much more collaborative and fun, and the work product even better.

Q: Your role demands attendance at a long list of PGA and golf-industry events. Do you ever tire of networking at conferences?

Sandy: Conferences and events have been very fruitful networking tools for me. I believe there is great value in external and internal conferencing, just as there is in internal and external networking. What I mean by that is, don't just attend conferences and events that are core or narrowly focused to your line of work or industry. Stretch beyond those boundaries and attend some that are adjacent to or possibly outside your field. You will find that your thinking will really be broadened and inspired when you get outside your regular line of business. For example, I recently went to the ADCOLOR Industry Conference. While this was a conference focused on diversity and inclusion, it was designed for professionals in creative and communications industries. It was tremendously beneficial to listen, learn, and view my diversity and inclusion efforts through a different lens. I found the attendees to be very willing to share insights, contact information, and a desire to connect postconference to further the dialogue and mutual interests.

Q: We initially connected because of a blog post I wrote for Levo.com. Generally, how do social networking platforms factor into the day-to-day of your job?

Sandy: I have found Twitter and LinkedIn to be tremendously powerful networking tools for my career and business development. I originally joined Twitter in 2009 to follow our corporate partners and stay up to speed on their breaking news and brand promotions. I discovered very quickly that the world was my oyster on Twitter. It is an unbelievable source of subject-matter expertise, emerging trends and topics, and individuals willing to share and lend support. While LinkedIn provides a more formal approach and a deeper dive, it serves the same purpose for me. So much of the business and professional development content I've sourced and so many of the professionals I work with I found by way of Twitter and LinkedIn.

You Can't Plan This

Networking is a process in which you engage. It's all about the effort you put in to build relationships and generously share your skills or expertise, know-how, and time. But ultimately all you can control are your own networking actions. And by controlling and directing your networking activities, you dramatically improve your chances of success.

I was an active member of the global business-networking group 85 Broads, much like its other members and local chapter leaders. My experience (becoming the network's first president) was different from that of other members because 85 Broads' founder, Janet Hanson, saw in my skills something that could benefit the network. I had the right skill set visible in the right place at the needed time. I had no control over that outcome beyond the networking effort I consistently put in.

2

Get Your Head in the Networking Game

ARE YOU SITTING up, ready to pay networking attention?

You're living in it, so you know it's a noisy, crowded, selfie-obsessed, me-me-me social world out there. Someone or another's crowdfunding campaign, career milestone, or new venture is competing for your attention, online and off, 24-7. Just responding to e-mail has become a full-time occupation. In 2015 the number of e-mails sent and received each day totaled over 205 billion. That number is predicted to reach 246 billion by 2019. E-mail volume (as it competes with new social communication channels) is an ongoing reminder of our communication challenges. Then there are all those other, disruptive ways to connect: The mobile-messaging service WhatsApp alone has processed 64 billion messages in a single day! And that's not counting the millions of video messages, photos, and voicemails sent through the WhatsApp platform (or the millions of communications exchanged on Slack, Trello, Paperless Post, or internal corporate networks).

Taping, texting, swiping, and clicking—we're at the intersection of unlimited access and fundamental economic shift.

And all this activity is being fueled by mobile technology and new business models, plus our very basic human need to forge bonds with other people. All that noise is a constant reminder that at any point in time, somewhere in your network someone needs money, insight, information, leads, expertise, introductions, favors, tweets, or some other response—immediately.

Your networking goal is to be heard through all that noise.

But first, you need to get your head into the new networking game with a few reminders about some old networking rules that, you shouldn't be too surprised to learn, are still relevant.

Expert Insight: Be Purposeful

Paying close attention to the behaviors of other people, along with having a clear focus on the primary task at hand, is one way to cut through all the networking noise. This is something executive recruiter Jennifer Johnson Scalzi does very well.

In 2004, Jennifer started a new job at a boutique search firm in New York City. All in all, her decision to accept the challenging, newly created position and relocate from Texas had taken about two weeks. It was a move she decided to make to advance her career: Jennifer knew no one other than her new boss (as a result of the interview process) before relocating (over the weekend before her job started). Within a few years, Jennifer was on a first-name basis with everyone (and I mean everyone) in the legal marketing industry. Rolling up her sleeves to get to know other people has been central to Jennifer's networked success.

Q: You didn't know anyone in New York City other than the person who just hired you, yet you took on the career challenge of moving to a new city and building a new business

line. What were you thinking? How did you approach this challenge?

Jennifer: I went at it with enthusiasm to soak in everything I could learn from my boss and those around me—from the way they answered their phones to how they greeted people in the office to where they took clients to lunch to how late they stayed and how early they arrived at the office. After a while I found my own work rhythm. I observed that the clients I needed to work closely with were often more available later in the day, so it made no sense for me to start making calls or sending e-mails before 9:30 a.m. if no-one picked up my messages until noon (or were ready to make time for a meeting until after 5:00 p.m.).

Q: New York City is full of professional obligations (events, meetups, conferences, dinners, happy hours) that can quickly become a distraction or complete waste of time. How did you sort out where to spend your networking time most productively?

Jennifer: At first I accepted every single invitation that was extended. Every. Single. One. I also made sure that everywhere I went I was either offering to help beforehand or during the event, or staying after to clean up. It didn't matter if it was professional or personal—I wasn't above handing out name tags at a reception or picking up dirty dishes—I wanted to be the invitee who was asked back again. On a practical business-networking note, when you're the one handing out name tags, you quickly transform yourself from "being new here" to knowing everyone on a first-name basis. By getting really involved and getting to know the event organizers, I was able to determine where I really needed to be spending my networking time.

Q: You have a deep, industry-focused network. How have you gone about expanding your professional connections into other fields? Why did you see the need to do that?

Jennifer: When I recognized my professional focus was so narrow, I made a deliberate effort to meet people other than recruiters and marketing professionals. I became actively involved with Dress for Success starting in 2010 (and then leading their junior advisory board in 2012). Other volunteers were young women from all walks of professional life: the fashion industry, Wall Street bankers, executives, and entrepreneurs. Because we were rallied around a cause we were all passionate about, we became fast friends and instantly expanded our networks as a direct result.

Q: What do you attribute your network-building success to?

Jennifer: The key is to know what people are capable of taking on and what's going on in their lives at any moment, so you know how you can help them or what you can reasonably ask them to do. Recognize that your networks are fluid—more active in some years, less in others. And learn to weed out the people who don't reciprocate early on!

Q: You started your career in Texas, and you've lived in New York City. Now, you're in Boston and your clients are located across the United States. How do you approach maintaining all your connections? What tools and suggestions do you have?

Jennifer: I have a birthday list and try to send cards to many people each year. I take a broad approach to social media. I follow everyone on Facebook and LinkedIn. I also use social media channels as a way to shoot a random note to say hi or check in. I've discovered sharing my own struggles and jubilations in my social media posts builds stronger bonds with my network, especially as I'm not seeing people in person on a regular basis. As I travel for work, I make sure that every time I visit a city I arrive with enough time to schedule one-on-one time with key relationships.

The Why Filter

One of the pieces of advice I regularly dish out is "Stop committing random acts of networking." Just as hope is not a strategy, random outreach is not an effective approach to problem solving, and at its core networking really is about seeking a solution to a problem or challenge you're facing.

Think about how you're approaching making connections now. How many times have you found yourself attending events and feeling you don't know why you're in the room (or why you got invited in the first place)? Or how many times have you declined to attend an office reception or holiday party because you figured it's just the folks in accounting who you can talk to any day, so why go? Did you succumb to FOMO (fear of missing out) and establish profiles on social media sites you rarely visit (other than to set up your profile)? The list of the random acts of networking we commit goes on and on.

Effective networking requires purpose and preparation. Anyone who is successfully navigating networking opportunities online and off knows why they wrote the blog or sent the tweet or accepted the invitation to the work reception. Jennifer's interview appears early in this chapter for that very reason! Her decision to accept every invitation when she moved to New

York City was far from random—it was quite purposeful: she needed to build a network in the legal marketing industry in order to do the job she was hired for!

Your first step to correct the course of your networking approach is to ask, Why?

And the answer to that "why?" equals:

- The end result you're seeking to achieve after all your networking efforts
- The problem you are looking to solve with the assistance of other people
- The direction you're headed in or the goal you want to reach—like a star quarterback looking down the field to the opposite end zone
- How you maintain your networking stamina as well as your focus
- The guardrail that keeps your efforts on track (and away from distractions and unnecessary schmoozing)
- The nagging question you are forced to answer before you fill every evening on your calendar with events you dread attending

Asking why saves your networking sanity and stops you from wasting valuable time and from worrying about missing out.

With Why, You Can Say Good-Bye to FOMO

Meetup, the largest network of local groups, helps more than nine thousand groups gather offline in local communities on a daily basis. CreativeMornings (a breakfast lecture series for the creative community) now meets in over 145 cities globally. On-line, LinkedIn welcomes two new members every second (and those members have over 1.4 million possible groups to join on the platform).

On a daily basis (or every second, if you stop to think about it) you are faced with endless networking choices—an abundance of opportunities to connect and exchange ideas. We're bombarded with *too many* opportunities (and choices between networking opportunities) most of the time. Fear of missing out is a networking distraction and feeds into networking fears. Don't let FOMO derail your focus!

Which is to say (again), this is why you need your why filter.

Asking why separates opportunity from a distracting time waste. When opportunities abound (meetups, Twitter chats, speed networking, reunions, summits, and seminars), how do you efficiently and quickly sort the productive from the less than productive? Here's the why filter I use:

- Is the opportunity aligned with my goal(s)?
- Will my participation add value to the other attendees and be valuable for me?
- Does the opportunity expand my network and/or strengthen existing relationships?
- What does my gut say? (Yes, I'm a big believer in trusting your gut.)

Having my why filter enables me to quickly reach yes or no decisions and to commit to networking opportunities without second-guessing FOMO. Knowing your why takes the gloss off a networking event when you realize the organizer's goals or planning acumen do not align with the outcomes you're seeking or connections you're hoping to make. The why filter enables you to be confidently happy with your decision about how and when to RSVP to an event.

One time, I flew over fifty-five hundred miles to speak on a mobile technology panel at a conference in Beirut. The distance (plus time zones and connecting flights) required me to block off an entire week to commit to this sixty-minute speaking opportunity. Seems a little crazy, but here's why I quickly agreed:

- Goal alignment: A goal for me in 2015 was to expand my network, and this was an audience I wanted to be in front of. The conference attracted a large audience of startups, investors, and key stakeholders in the growing tech ecosystem. Although I was well known as an investor, startup advisor, and advocate for women entrepreneurs in the New York City tech community, this conference presented me with the opportunity to expand my reputation beyond Silicon Alley.

- Value add: My only hesitation in accepting the invitation to speak on the conference-opening "Hot Trends in Web and Mobile" panel was whether my investment experience in mobile technologies and insights from being an active observer of mobile trends would be helpful to the attendees. Doing something that scared me, such as reaching beyond my expertise comfort zone, fueled my research on mobile trends prior to the conference.

- Expanding my network: Again, this opportunity exposed me to a new startup and investor audience. I had not traveled to the region previously. My networking with friends and contacts in Egypt and Dubai relied heavily on technology (Skype, Google Hangouts, FaceTime). While social media platforms and good old e-mail have offered up ways to maintain my few valuable connections, at the end of the day no networking is complete without personal, direct introductions and face-to-face conversations. As my friend and mentor Frank Kimball would say: "Until you take the final step of connecting—personally, old school— the network is incomplete and useless."

- Gut reaction. One lesson I've learned from my investing activities and career choices is never doubt your gut. My gut told me to say yes based on the source of the referral. I was recommended as a speaker to the Beirut-based conference organizers by a Cairo-based entrepreneur I've known for a number of years—and, frankly, I don't know if there is a more genuine compliment than to be recommended by someone who values your opinion, understands your professional ambitions, and is seeking to help you out. The recommendation was a networking win-win.

Opportunities don't come to those who hesitate or dither or endlessly ask questions before making a decision. Or as my friend Alison Levine, author of the *New York Times* best-seller *On the Edge*: *Leadership Lessons from Mount Everest and Other Extreme Environments*, said to me in an e-mail exchange:

> *You can't just sit back and think magic will happen—you gotta enthusiastically wave your wand, put some tricks up your sleeve.*

Determining your why filter enables you to enthusiastically wave your wand while everyone else is hesitating or waiting to see if there is a better offer. Asking why is all about taking control and putting yourself in front of opportunities. Yes, I've missed a few, but when I think of the alternative—wasting my time, being in front of the wrong audience, being out of pocket for the cost of a registration fee—having a why filter enables me to cancel noise, peel back distraction, and assess whether what is before me really is the right opportunity for me right now.

Connect like an Introvert

In the course of writing this book, I discovered that many of the people I selected to interview were introverts. This really surprised me. When I chose who to interview, I was only focused on those who achieved their desired outcomes by establishing strong relationships through concerted networking efforts. I instinctively looked to people I admired for the ways they connected and achieved goals they had set for themselves. Personality type had absolutely not crossed my mind.

Manisha Thakor is one of those profoundly introverted people who has addressed her dislike of networking by taking control of the process. And Manisha now views making "human connections" as the most important part of her business day. Manisha is the director of wealth strategies for women at the BAM Alliance, a community of 140-plus independent registered investment advisors. Listening to an interview with Zig Ziglar transformed her fear of networking. As she recalls, "Zig said something along the lines of 'You can get whatever you want in life if you will just first help others get whatever they want,' and this notion of helping others felt more comfortable to me than the idea of networking as 'schmoozing.'"

Manisha has grown her wealth-management business one small networking event at a time. Her aim with each event—from her Lean In Ladies Lunches to Playing Big evening receptions—has been to make connections to help every attendee solve a problem or address a business challenge. Of course, gaining new clients was her ultimate goal, but Manisha pursues her particular goal by being helpful and continually at the top of her network's mind. And let's face it, achieving your goal (while also helping others achieve theirs), does drastically reduce networking anxiety.

After holding many networking events over the years, Manisha offers up these success tips:

- **Select attendees carefully.** Initially Manisha invited everyone she met or was referred to (a strategy similar to Jennifer's). Over time Manisha got a better sense of the type of person she needed to extend an invitation to. Ultimately, knowing exactly who she was looking to meet opened up opportunities to invite more of the potential clients she was looking for.
- **Have an actionable takeaway.** Manisha's goal for each event is for the attendees to walk away with investing information they can put to use right away. Her second goal is for attendees to have a solid understanding of what services her firm offers. And, yes, Manisha does tell people up front that she's growing her business.
- **Create a follow-up strategy.** Manisha has a monthly newsletter-distribution list that she adds attendees to. About once a month, she also circulates some of the best articles she has found on women's empowerment and personal finance as well as other new resources or interesting books.
- **Build your network early.** Early on in Manisha's career someone told her to establish a network long before she ever needed one. Knowing it takes time to establish trust, Manisha's guidance is to start building relationships early and to keep at it!

Expert Insight: Be the Host

She's the best-selling author of *Cooking Up a Business*,[13] worked as a food editor at *O, The Oprah Magazine*, and created an online PR course, but at her core Rachel Hofstetter is the perfect host.

It is in her DNA. She excels at the magic of bringing the right people together. So it is no wonder then that she founded a technology startup, Guesterly (acquired in 2015 by photo-book subscription service Chatbooks), focused on extending the warm hand of the host by connecting guests before a big event.

You may never host an event but your networking efforts will benefit by thinking like you are. A tip I offer introverts or those who generally feel ill at ease when they walk into crowded receptions or conference venues is "be the host." By assuming the mind-set of the host even when it's not your party, meetup, or event, you tend to stop focusing on how you're feeling at that very moment, because now you're interested in the well-being of others in the room. By making others feel more comfortable, you'll make yourself more at ease too.

Q: You're the guest specialist and your startup Guesterly is focused on facilitating faster, easier connections for guests at events. Describe the attributes of a great host.

Rachel: A great host makes everyone feel like an honored guest: it sounds obvious, but being delighted to see each person (from your best friend to a plus-one) goes a long way.

A great host also acts as "social lubricant," dropping a few conversation starters along with the guest introduction. ("Jody is the fastest runner between here and Texas, and you should ask her about the time she debated the governor.") It never hurts to have a few fun facts or questions handy, to help get people out of their shells.

A great host also enjoys their own party! Switch out of "planner" mode before people arrive, so you can be in full-on, in-the-party-moment host mode.

Q: What are your tips for making an event welcoming for all the guests?

Rachel: Sharing details on things like logistics makes people feel comfortable and prepared. Think through how someone will approach your event from start to finish, with an eye on where you'd want information: what will they wear, how will they get there, who will they see, what will they eat or drink, etc. This makes guests feel intrinsically welcome and at ease before they even walk in the door. For example, will your party have light bites, heavier food, or just drinks? Or let out-of-towners know that the nearest subway line doesn't run on Saturdays or that your event is located on a one-way street.

At your event, focus on first impressions: how a guest feels in those initial moments shapes their whole event. A warm greeting from the host, an easy place to put bags and coats, and offering a drink go a long way. If at all possible, bring newcomers over to other partygoers and introduce them to someone they can start talking to—this takes away that awkward moment of "who should I talk to?" while making guests feel like VIPs.

Finally, find the person standing alone—you'll make their day when you bring them into a conversation. And this tip works regardless of whether you're the host or an attendee: the easiest way to make a new friend at an event is to go talk to that person who feels just as alone or awkward as you do. You're solving your problem and theirs at the same time—win-win!

Q: Events such as weddings are temporary communities that come together around a milestone. What are your suggestions for enhancing the connections in these situations (and which in turn may be applied to other situations)?

Rachel: The community that can form at events like weddings is truly powerful: someone you love has gathered everyone they love in one place, and so we end up being more open to making new connections. To help facilitate those connections, hosts can do three easy things:

1. **Appoint ambassadors.** There will always be some attendees who fall outside the normal "circles" and don't know very many people. Ask a well-connected guest to be their "ambassador" at the event and to introduce and include them.

2. **Create carpools.** If people are traveling from the same city to your event (either via car, public transport, or plane), take ten minutes to connect them via e-mail. This simple connection means people show up already thinking this is a great event.

3. **Help people know who's who.** Simply being able to remember a new name creates stronger connections, as studies show that we're less likely to talk to an acquaintance if we can't remember his or her name! Don't let that get in the way of your guests: give them help with names and faces. It can be as polished as a guest directory, or I've seen name tags and buttons with each person's connection to the host, event, or couple, and even a Google Doc with a list of guests and links to their Twitter profiles.

Q: How does online networking download into the "real" world for you? Is there a distinction anymore between networking online and networking offline?

Rachel: I love online networking. Online networking is a great way to start (or follow up and continue) a relationship, but it's most effective when there's some "real world" interaction in there too—even if real world is a phone date! And you don't need to be meeting IRL all the time: I've found that even once every year or two keeps a relationship healthy if you have some online contact in the interim.

More or Less?

A *New York Times* article, "Out of the Loop in Silicon Valley,"[14] caught my eye back in 2010—and sticks with me still today. The article stated:

> Networks are crucial for fund-raising, because most investors don't look at pitches that come over the transom.

I remember thinking, when I finished reading the article: networks are crucial—period, full stop.

Whether it is funding a startup, finding a job, landing a board seat, learning more about your child's school, getting the name of good trainer, launching your business, or asking for restaurant recommendations—all of these activities depend on networks. To get things done in this hyperconnected world, you need, more often than not, to access to a wide range of people, with varying experiences and backgrounds. And you need to be able to tap in to this knowledge network regularly.

Investors in emerging technology companies are just one narrow segment of my network. For me, deep networks of close friends, mentors, and advisors are needed for feedback, guidance, and advice. Then broad, expansive networks are needed to connect to new opportunities and ideas that are outside the knowledge base or expertise of my close, inner circle. Recognize, as I have, that you need both types of networks, and recognize that you'll use these networks differently.

The *New York Times* article also went on to say:

> Women tend to network with women, and men tend to network with men . . . It plays out on the golf course, in the boardroom and it's certainly playing out in high-growth entrepreneurship.

Here's my advice:

- Network with women.
- Network with men.
- Network up the corporate ladder, down it, and across it—as well as with your peers and competitors.
- Network with people outside your professional field, social circle, age demographic, and geographic location.

Remember, good ideas—like invitations to speak at conferences thousands of miles away—can come from anywhere, so throw your networking attitude far and wide. Don't wait till you need to (such as moving to a new city) to start actively networking. You're limiting your opportunities—and access to good ideas and advice—when you limit the radius of your networks.

More or Less: Which Is Your Network?

I want you to stop for a second and answer this question: does your current network support your ambitions?

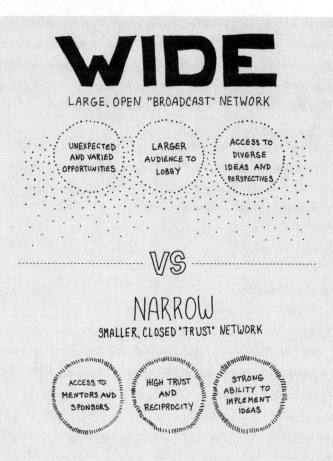

The type of network you have will either float your idea or sink your dream—it all depends on the types of people in your contact list or address book.

Is your network a tight community of like-minded peers? If so, chances are you're highly successful at implementing an idea or getting a task accomplished because you have a trusted group of colleagues to turn to in order to get the job done. Does your network stretch across time zones and industries, as well as skill sets and job titles? You're definitely in the right place to test a theory, introduce a novel idea, or rally for a cause. And while that broad or wide network puts you in the epicenter of diverse information flows, don't dismiss the importance of also having a narrow network: that closely held community keeps one another top-of-mind and has one another's backs when it comes to promotion or career advancement.

Too much of one and not enough of the other in your network? Now you know where you need to start focusing your relationship-building efforts.

Time Won't Give You Time

"I don't have enough time to network." This is the biggest excuse out there. And really what it says is:

- I don't have time for other people, and
- I won't make the time to invest in myself.

No one has been able to hack more hours from a day or days from the week, so how do you find time to network when you're constantly being pulled in different directions by work, family, friends, and other social commitments?

Reframe your belief about what networking really is!

By reframing, you'll see that those tasks you undertake daily can be supreme networking opportunities. Small changes in your daily routine can set you apart and lead to big opportunities. It all depends on your focus: Are you talking about your work? Are you excited and asking for new clients or opportunities? One attorney I know, while awaiting a pickup at day care, decided to chat with another parent about something other than their children, and it led to an important new corporate client.

TIME WON'T ⏰ GIVE YOU TIME

However, taking time to...

Strike up a conversation with another parent (while waiting in line at day care pickup) may land you a new corporate client.

Walk down the hall to continue a conversation with an office colleague off e-mail and in lieu of a call will likely result in you scoring a key internal champion.

Write a 600-word blog post could land you a speaking engagement. *(Yes, this is how I met Sandy Cross and was invited to the PGA Championship.)*

Networking should not be considered the "other" activity you'll get to or make a priority when you "have more time." Even if work demands being at your desk 24-7, there are microchances to network in meaningful ways, and they can be as simple as writing a short note.

Lawyers account for their time by the hour or, more accurately, by the sixth of an hour—a fact I know all too well. The need to put in long hours to meet the deadline imposed by a demanding client is a terrific professional excuse not to get out from behind a desk and meet people (including your own colleagues), but flipping out of that mind-set is crucial for career success (as well as for creating great personal satisfaction with one's career); and no one in the profession knows this better than Lois Herzeca.

Lois is a partner at the global law firm Gibson, Dunn & Crutcher, where she coheads the firm's fashion and retail practice group. Lois and I initially met as members of an advisory board to an organization focused on advancing women in the legal profession. With her deep fashion-industry expertise and her willingness to mentor and support women entrepreneurs in New York City's vibrant fashion startup community, Lois and I further connected in mutually beneficial ways as my own career detoured away from law and into emerging technology companies. When I was planning a networking event that featured a prominent founder of a fashion-tech startup as keynote speaker, Lois was my first call to host the event.

A simple networking example with a big career impact from early in Lois's career didn't even require her to leave her desk.

As a young law-firm partner with two small children, Lois joined the board of a new nonprofit encouraging children to help other children who were in need. She learned about the nonprofit from a brochure that managed to find its way onto her desk. Lois was impressed with what she read, so she wrote the not-for-profit a small check, sending it along with a personal note expressing her interest in getting involved. The note lead to a call from the organization's founder, then to an in-person meeting, and ultimately to Lois's decision to join the board. This was her first board membership and has led to other board positions and the many important business contacts that frequently come with being in such positions. If Lois had simply sent the check, without the note, she might have missed out on what became a very fulfilling and productive part of her professional (and personal) life.

Here's a simple way for you to start reframing daily tasks into relationship-building opportunities: if you work in the same office, rather than continue a conversation with a colleague via e-mail or instant message or on speakerphone, walk down the hall to her or his office to have that chat. Chances are you'll deepen the relationship and gain more information from the face-to-face encounter.

Saying No

Sometimes you've just got to put your foot down and say no— no to skipping an event because a client or colleague has announced a new project deadline, no to tagging along because a friend has said, "It will be fun. You should go."

Here's the key: understand why you're saying no.

Goals are your why filter when you're weighing which new networking event or relationship to pursue. By staying focused on where you're headed, you'll be able to figure out whether saying no will get you further ahead or is simply an excuse that's holding you back.

Guesterly's Rachel Hofstetter focuses her networking efforts by keeping both her long-term and shorter-term goals in mind. When she was getting ready to raise investment money, Rachel prioritized attending investor and startup-focused events. At other times (such as when she was launching her online PR school or beta testing a new feature on Guesterly), Rachel focused on expanding into new networking circles. Just as Jennifer Johnson Scalzi did, when Rachel moved to a new city, she found herself attending every type of event she could, in order to meet people. Expanding her network was why she accepted every invitation and checked out every event, rather than turning them down. When she launched Guesterly into the wedding market (an industry where she previously knew no one), she attended every wedding-industry-related event she could find, in order to figure out exactly where she needed to focus her networking efforts.

Sometimes saying no gets you closer to—yes, you guessed it—your ultimate goal.

Saying No to No

We've all done it: tossed the embossed card in the trash or skipped clicking on the link sent via Eventbrite or deleted the Paperless Post invitation, without a second thought. Bombarded by requests, the natural knee-jerk response is often simply to say no.

But hold on!

Are there networking events you should never say no to?

Yes, these do exist, especially in the workplace. Universally saying you will never attend networking events at work is—not to be too dramatic here—career suicide. Never say no to opportunities to get to know your peers and colleagues.

Job pressures and competition keep too many of us in our cubicles from the moment we step off the elevator to the minute we dash to the train. One Wall Street investment banker I knew regularly ordered in pizza for his group as a way to bring the team together. This was no "free" lunch: pizza was ordered (and he happily paid for it each week) on the condition that no one could eat alone. It doesn't take much to break down communication barriers and build team rapport. In twenty minutes you can accomplish more than consuming a slice or two of pizza—you can build relationships.

My friend Varelie Croes is a former director of international tax financial services at PricewaterhouseCoopers. During her eleven years at the firm, she organized many events and ran a number of different initiatives for one simple reason: it was a great way to meet people and connect with leadership in the firm. Varelie knows that her volunteer efforts expedited her career trajectory within PwC. Once colleagues worked with her on a project (even a voluntary one), Varelie noticed she was being requested for more projects and staffed on the best deals; plus she was invited to an increasing number of events typically limited to more senior leadership. Her participation also resulted in more external speaking opportunities, where her expertise (and PwC's reputation) could really shine. Varelie's promotion to director in 2003 was a "fast-tracked" one—an outcome she credits to the network she built within the firm.

Saying no to attending work-related networking events is like telling someone that keeping your head down and doing good work will get you ahead in the workplace or that salary increases are the result of good karma. Of course you need to be strategic and sometimes rather selective in which work-related networking events you choose to attend, but don't apply a universal no to opportunities to share your knowledge with colleagues beyond the radius of your cubicle, or to being further informed of developments in your chosen profession.

There are many, many, many ways to limit your career opportunities; take "no to networking" off that list.

Look Both Ways

Networking is a two-way street. You've likely heard this all-too-frequently-tossed-out phrase before, but what does it really mean?

It is about putting your own goals aside for just a moment and remembering that everyone else has goals, time commitments, and priorities too. Simple, right? It's understanding that there are times when you need to hold back on requesting a favor or plan to take a longer, indirect networking route because that key contact you've relying on is now too busy with a project of her own to help you.

What you should realize by now is that, more often than not, networking is about being surrounded by the right group of people to help you. It's finding the "give, give, get" people (as Rachel Hofstetter refers to them) and becoming one too.

Who are "give, give, get" people? Look around; they are the people in your network who:

- Use their networks to solve someone else's problem
- Anticipate needs and ask, "What can I do to help you?"
- Follow up on the introduction, tip, or lead

- Keep tabs on what is important to you—even if it's simply a like or favorite or share on a social networking site
- Follow through (or tell you why the timing won't work for them)
- Get you an answer (even if the answer is not the one you were hoping for)

Being successful at networking is realizing that to get where you're going you need to help others get to where they are going too.

It's Not About You

"I love texting. You don't have to get anyone on the phone."

I made a mental note of this comment as soon as I overheard it, not because I was speaking with someone who was sharing their communication preferences (which the speaker clearly was), but rather because this statement (said by a young woman to her grandmother) clearly illustrated the point that all networking interactions are about understanding the other person. And, yes, the grandmother was in absolute agreement about the efficiency of texting.

Who is the decision maker whose attention you are trying to get? Are they a golfer? An opera fan? A power user of Facebook Messenger? You may have identified the individual or group you need to connect with, but have you paid attention to how they interact? You may love emoji texts (or handwritten thank-you notes), but what's the communication preference of the person you're trying to reach?

Every interaction is a chance to observe and to build that

ever-so-essential networking element of trust. The upside to the new, noisy networking landscape is that most of us leave a distinct trail of interests, more than just a hint of communication preferences, along with our hobbies and passions. There is no need to guess: just sift through and pay attention to all of this networking data!

Be Network Minded

Studies have shown that helping others is good for your health and can actually be addictive (the "helper's high"), but helping others is also good for advancing your career and improving your company's bottom line. Cisco Systems, a worldwide leader in IT, knows this. Cisco's Intranet Strategy Group recognized back in 2006 that it needed to find a better way of connecting employees, groups, and information. Two years later, it released a connections-centric directory aimed at enhancing teamwork, collaboration, and networking across the company. By facilitating information flow, Cisco is also discovering who in the company are the connectors: employees who, not based on title or hierarchy or pay scale, are the bridges between people, ideas, and new opportunities. Information in large organizations like Cisco tends to be siloed, and unblocking those communication channels is a game-changing business opportunity.

This exact same opportunity exists in your day-to-day interactions with your network. Perhaps you're one of those people who have strong networks of friends, family, and coworkers, not to mention the people you regularly see at the gym, church, day care, or volunteer group. Then there is all that technology that enables us to assemble lots of contacts (and with mobile, easy 24-7 connectivity to them all). But simply being online and accessible, with lots of friends, followers, and connections, is not going to change your networking game, as it is often not much more than accumulating a bigger online version of a physical address book.

Switch from being ready to network to being network minded. Use your network to solve someone else's problem.

Here's how to start cultivating a "network-minded" reputation:

- Listen and find out what other people are interested in. This includes listening online!
- Provide critical information, expertise, or connections to get someone closer to the critical information or expertise they are seeking.
- Share resources and become a source of information about issues and opportunities in your school, workplace, or extended social community.
- Share your influence, even if you have only a little.
- Cultivate a willingness to continue making relationships and to pass on information.

Carry the Trust Torch

Next to generosity, trust is essential to building strong relationships successfully. So, how do you build trust in a hyperconnected world?

- Silence notifications and put down your mobile phone.
- Close your laptop.

- Power off your tablet.
- Step away from your desktop.

An unconnected network is useless because you are unlikely to build a solid foundation of trust simply on the basis of a text or a tweet. How many times have you scratched your head after reading an e-mail, completely lost as to context, nuance, and personality?

Joe Styler, aftermarket product manager at GoDaddy, works in an almost completely virtual environment, regularly communicating with clients and potential clients through instant messages and e-mails, yet even for Joe this is not sufficient to land the big deals. Face-to-face meetings are essential for doing his job. Even for a business at the heart of this interconnected economy, people will only do business with those they know and trust—and trust is built face-to-face.

Tina Roth Eisenberg and her eight-person team at Creative-Morning's headquarters built a 145-city (and growing) community on the strength of volunteer leaders working together virtually. However, Tina noticed an uptick in collaboration (plus vastly improved e-mail communications) after a host summit in New York City was organized for all these leaders from thirty-seven different countries. As Tina described it to me, communications among the volunteers changed completely after the summit, becoming friendlier, more trustful, and self-regulating. All because they had met together in one physical room—and this was a community of like-minded people with shared experiences to start with!

Networking is about connecting with people and, yes, some of my greatest friendships started with an online connection—

as I like to joke, "I'm the girl you meet on Twitter." But the friendships were only solidified when we met offline—on Skype or at a meetup or over a meal.

Connected people use their relationship capital generously to help people they know and trust. Trust remains the critical piece of all successful networking efforts. Tap, swipe, and try as they might, apps, algorithms, and smart technology cannot seem to establish or disrupt the essential networking foundation of trust.

Another Reminder to Share

A 2010 *New York Times* article on the power of collaboration caught my attention. The article was on Alzheimer's research and highlighted the results of a global effort to find the biological markers that show the progression of the disease.[15] The fruit of these research efforts was the result of a collaborative and connected effort that brought together scientists, pharmaceutical companies, and governments. Various stakeholders sharing information and results! The participants in the research effort willingly and openly shared all their data and findings with one another, plus made all this information public—immediately.

What's remarkable about this scientific effort in a networking context? Surprisingly, there was no precedent for this sort of global, collaborative, connected effort: no prior practice of working together, connecting the stakeholders, aligning interests, and parking egos at the door. The old research model was siloed—structured around scientists doing their own research, with their own patients, and using their own methods. The old model did not facilitate information flow, resulting in little visible progress to understanding the progression of this disease (which in turn meant research-funding issues). The lack of medical progress on this disease shifted when the siloed research model was replaced with a connected one.

Sharing information generously with your network may not have the same world-changing results; however, chances are you can achieve something more powerful by connecting with others. Don't be a hoarder of information; share it and make something happen with it.

3

How and Where to Start

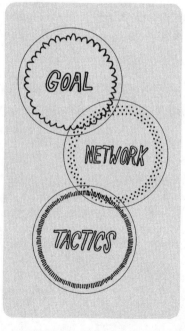

WITH SOME OF THE "OLD" RULES of networking behind us, as well as a refresher on the networking values to hold on to, it's time to think about where you want your relationships to take you. Knowing where you're headed is essential to making the connections you need. Pick a career, life, or new-business target—it's time to focus your networking on the connections and activities that will move you closer to achieving that goal.

If you're reading this book, I know you're not the type who wants to wait for introductions or dumb luck to kick in. You're ready to take control of your networking destiny. And you know it's time to stop being distracted by photo-sharing platforms, dazzled by the endless array of meetup options, and confused by which tactics to use to deepen connections and ignite your goals.

Congratulations—you've unchecked the networking excuse box labeled "I know I have to do this but don't know where to start, so I'll procrastinate further."

Networking efforts need to start with a focus—a direction to head in—or else you're just randomly schmoozing. When you're networking, it's all about aiming your efforts toward your goal and staying focused on what it is you are trying to achieve along the way. What's the next career milestone you're aiming for? What's the passion project you've always wanted to launch? What's your goal that needs community support to get off the ground?

Setting a goal gets you started by putting you in control and out of networking anxiety's way. After establishing your goal, identifying the connections who can help you will provide the necessary momentum to move your goal along.

This is how you end random acts of networking!

The Goal Comes First

As I've said from the start, I believe there are connection-based solutions for pretty much every challenge we face in our jobs and careers, whether it is finding a job, securing a donation, or locating a source. Sorry, your problems aren't new—someone has faced your dilemma before (or a challenge that looks an awful lot like it) or knows someone who has—and this is good news! You now have the chance to leverage their mistakes and insights to improve your own networked outcome.

Looking back at my career and goals (secure a job in New York City, transition out of law practice into legal management, find a literary agent), it's evident that I've continually followed a process, taking logical steps to move from having a need or idea or desire to achieving the end result.

My problem-solving process looks like this:

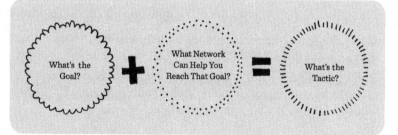

As I hinted in chapter 1, it's a process that:

- starts with setting a goal
- requires determining the correct connections or network to ask for help
- and then focuses on strategy and communication tactics after you've figured out whom you're seeking help from.

Remember I mentioned in chapter 1 how I hate walking into rooms filled with strangers? If I walk into a room of strangers, it means I don't know why I'm in that room. I'm unprepared. I'm unfocused. I don't have a goal to ground my busyness! And starting the networking process without having a focus or a goal only fuels networking anxiety.

Lacking focus means you run the risk of pursuing aimless networking activities and constantly questioning the value of networking events, which in turn fuels impatience with networking, a feeling that it is not working, and so on and so on—eventually leading you down an unproductive, time-wasting spiral of networking unhappiness.

Expert Insights: Landing the Postcollege Dream Job

Jessica Peltz-Zatulove is a Madison Avenue veteran turned venture capitalist. She's been named one of New York City's "100 Most Influential People in Tech" by *TechWeek* and has appeared on CNBC, Fox Business, and popular startup podcasts *BroadMic* and *The Pitch Deck*. The career path of dreams, right? Actually it's a career cultivated one researched, intentional networking step and new connection at a time. Because, you see, back in 2002 Jessica was a graduate from the Kelley School of Business at Indiana University Bloomington and seeking her first job. While Jessica is highly connected in New York City today, that was not her story back in 2002 when she had ambition but no industry connections and one big goal—to land a job!

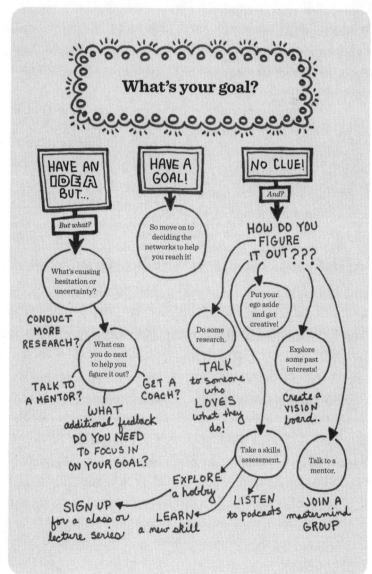

Q: **You were initially convinced, after a series of job interviews, that after college your career would be in Chicago. When that fell through, you bounced back by setting your focus on a career in New York City. Can you describe how you approached finding a job in a city where you had no contacts?**

Jessica: After having an internship at a top media agency in Chicago, I was in the final round of interviews with the global media agency Starcom. I was convinced I would get the job. Momentarily devastated when I got a rejection letter instead, I reset my career-ambition compass and moved to New York City. That was in 2002, not too long after 9/11 plus the dot-com bubble, so I was entering an uncertain job market and I needed to be strategic.

I began my media-agency job search by subscribing to *Ad Age* (plus getting my hands on every other printed trade publication out there). I had to not only understand New York advertising agencies but, more important, just like in the series *Mad Men*, I needed to know who was winning new business from the big brands.

Here's what I did:

- I studied where the client accounts were moving between advertising agencies. Then I researched the names of the executives who were being quoted or recruited away as a result of landing the new business.
- I created a handwritten notebook of the news and updates from every major agency. LinkedIn was new and not the information-rich platform it is today, so I managed my research efforts the old-fashioned way: highlighting news articles and using Post-it notes!

▪ Armed with all this industry intelligence, I sent my résumé, together with a customized cover letter, to the senior executives I had researched, congratulating them on winning the new business, then pointing out their need to be staffing up to manage the new client account.

Q: That's a rather thoughtful way to attack the job-search challenge. You were obviously successful in landing that first job in New York. What's your advice for job seekers who are reaching out "cold" to land a job interview? Any suggestions on how to connect when you don't have that critical warm introduction?

Jessica: In today's hyperconnected world, it's much easier to research not only the person you want to meet but also who in your network can make a warm introduction. Many people openly express their opinions online (via traditional media or blogs or social networks), so job seekers have the advantage of understanding the person they want to meet (i.e., what the person is passionate about, what their area of expertise is, and what career path they took to get where they are). It is a research exercise to find common points of interest or ways to be helpful. And these small details are the ones that raise interest in an introductory e-mail.

Reflecting back on my postcollege experience, here are some ways I'd approach a job search now:

▪ Follow the person on Twitter and Snapchat.
▪ See who you might have as a common connection on LinkedIn and ask for an introduction.
▪ Follow the person's personal or corporate blog or Tumblr or posts on Medium. Find where they express an opinion

and read all of it. If a busy person is taking the time to put their thoughts online in a blog post, the subject matter probably is important to them, so read it all!

- Leverage your college alumni network. As a graduate of Indiana University Bloomington I have a community of over six hundred thousand graduates to tap into. That is an amazing resource for job leads and business introductions.
- Set up a Google alert for when companies or individuals are mentioned in the press.
- Attend events or panels when you discover the person you want to meet is scheduled to be speaking. While you can learn a lot about a person from what is posted online, seeing how they interact with an audience or speak off-the-cuff may reveal so much more.

Q: Generosity is a key element of successful networking efforts. What does it mean to you in the job-search context? What guidance do you have for others on being generous in an era when so many people are looking for the next gig or opportunity or promotion?

Jessica: Networking generosity at any stage of the job search is about communicating regularly with the people who are going out of their way to help you. For job seekers, I always recommend keeping people in the loop so they can share in the joy of your success and progress along the way. If you're the person who made a connection for someone that ultimately led to success in landing a new job (or internship or client), you don't want to hear this great news from a third party.

Q: How has your postcollege approach to landing a job influenced subsequent networking efforts in your career (or the advice you provide others)?

Jessica: It taught me to take risks and believe there's a bigger opportunity out there. If I'm interested in something, I'll explore it through research and networking, instead of thinking I probably won't get the job.

Zigging and Zagging

If you hadn't read the previous pages, it might appear that my career in the startup community has (much like Jessica's) accelerated quickly—overnight, you might say, which it has in many ways—but the bigger reality about my current success is the backstory, the years of building relationships and tackling challenges in a purposeful, deliberate, networked way. Mine is an ongoing story of community-fueled reinvention, of being able to take career steps forward by stepping backward (or, more often than not, sideways) and continually tapping into my connections for feedback and guidance.

I no longer see career success as following a defined, lockstep path (as I did in my early career as an attorney). For me, it's about continually and intentionally creating connections so I can pursue new interests and career directions. It's about having a network so I can deliberately take risks and put myself in front of more and evolving opportunities.

Get Comfortable with Being Uncomfortable

There is comfort in predictability, much like a reliable Internet connection. And most of us like sticking to routines. Taking the same route to the subway. Seeing the Starbucks barista who gets our latte order right every morning (or magically misspells our name each time). Routine seems to indicate the correctly managed progression of a task or having control over a project. If we just got into the routine, things would move forward.

Because if it's not routine, then it's change—and change is something a lot of people have an absurd fear of. Whether it is a career transition, a move, or a departmental reorganization, these are life events that come with challenging decisions and all sorts of uncertainty until things settle down into a new routine.

But thanks to disruptive technology and the slow economic recovery after 2007, uncertainty and change really are the markers of the world we now live in. Change is the new routine—and you might just want to get comfortable with that because in all this upheaval you'll likely discover your greatest strengths (as well as some unique, game-changing opportunities).

Claudia Batten does not shy away from change. She's recognized that it is where she thrives, where she really performs at her best. You could say she has cultivated a passion for seeking the uncomfortable flow of change.

Claudia is a serial entrepreneur. Her career started on a predictable path—college to corporate office—until she packed up and moved to New York City from her native New Zealand in 2002. She arrived in the Big Apple three months after 9/11, with no fixed plan and without any job prospects. I remember the job-market uncertainty back then—everyone was firing, no one was hiring. A rational impulse at that time would have been to pack up and go home to New Zealand, with fingers crossed that she'd get her old job back.

And if Claudia had been seeking a job, she might have done just that. Claudia's really big dream, however, was not to just land a j-o-b but to be part of the Internet revolution. Start a company when everyone around you is downsizing or closing down? Who would face the uncertainty of doing that? Claudia.

Embracing failure and uncertainty as opportunities (as well as occupational realities if she was going pursue this line of work), Claudia rustled up every ounce of her ambition and went on to become part of the founding team of not one but two successful technology startups. Her first was a gaming startup called Massive, which sold to Microsoft in 2006. Then Havas acquired a majority stake in her second startup in 2012 (Victors & Spoils, an advertising agency built on the principles of crowd-sourcing). Instead of easing into a comfortable offline office routine after each acquisition, Claudia chose to continue pursuing the discomfort by accepting new challenges as her next goals.

Looking back, Claudia sees that her career success is all about navigating the uncertainty that comes with making choices in a world not measured in timely promotions and defined titles or the prospect of lifetime employment with a single, stable employer.

But when you think about how so many people make a living now—freelance or project-based work, temporary assignments, passion projects, side gigs, and advisory roles—it's about zigging and zagging, toggling multiple tasks, and cobbling together experiences that create a career (and at the same time a life). It's most definitely uncomfortable at times. But as I see it, Claudia's outside-the-safety-zone career path looks more and more like a regular career routine now.

And, really, who wants to stuff themselves into a structured career box for forty years when it is now possible to connect to opportunities and design a unique career future instead?

So how do you take bold steps and leap into career uncertainty—in good times or in bad? By making strong connections a daily to-do-list priority.

Claudia attributes her success to cultivating great networks. Connections have been critical to her career momentum, combined with her clear focus on what she wants to achieve next. Regardless of how uncomfortable it is at times, her advice is to keep taking steps forward—it may be the tiny actions that ignite opportunity and move an ambitious goal forward. And you can take every one of those steps if you have a network.

As for Claudia, she's currently working on yet another tech startup (the mobile app Broadli) while also focusing on reinventing the relationship between a traditionally bureaucratic government function and the startup constituency it serves (new territory for her career indeed). Claudia was appointed the regional director of the New Zealand Trade and Enterprise North America office in 2015, tasked with bringing her unique experience to the table as the office reimagines how best to connect New Zealand entrepreneurs to the US market. No certainty that she'll succeed as she has in her past efforts, but that's the point of pushing yourself, isn't it?

Look to Your Network to Ignite Your Career

You've likely heard the advice "dress for the job you want, not for the job you have" more than once or twice before. It's excellent guidance on communicating to your network how you want to be perceived. But have you ever stopped to observe how your network sees you now?

Since my career has zigged and zagged, my connections have watched me switch a number of professional hats (or wear several at the same time). It is not unusual for me to receive "what are you up to now?" e-mails. Based on what I've shared online and my IRL interactions, I've been referred to over the years as a:

- Founder
- Accelerator
- Investor
- Startup advisor
- Advisory board member
- Board member
- Catalyst
- Connector
- Serial connector
- Master networker
- Networker
- Project manager
- People manager
- Social media influencer
- Online reputation builder
- Twitter aficionado
- Network activator
- Relationship builder
- Strategic thinker and doer
- Mentor
- Sponsor
- Speaker
- Moderator
- Keynote speaker
- Force of nature

Some are labels, a few are real titles, and others are just stuff I know I do very well. Because of a 360-degree performance review back in 2007, I discovered I was a very well-respected departmental manager and my true career passion was in rolling up my sleeves to get things done. (Career tip: take full advantage of self-assessments and performance reviews to understand what motivates you!) As I look back at the ways my connections describe me now—doer, force of nature, network activator—I'm somewhat amused at how completely risk-averse I was in my career until 2009. Why do others see us better than we see ourselves?

If only I'd asked my network for feedback or paid attention to how they saw me earlier in my career . . .

Think about this: the path your career will take is directly related to the people now interacting with you on a day-to-day basis. Observe how they respond to you. If in doubt, seek their input, ask for feedback. See what your network sees in you, as you may just find your next opportunity in the process. For in many ways, we're interviewing for our next great career with every post, handshake, and membership affiliation (constantly remind yourself of this before you hit Send on an e-mail or before you hastily brush aside the value of a new networking opportunity).

The Eighteen-Month Career Transition Success Story

Back in 2001 I experienced my first real career itch. I knew it was time to make a change, but to what, exactly?

My first networking goal was to discover what I wanted to make of myself.

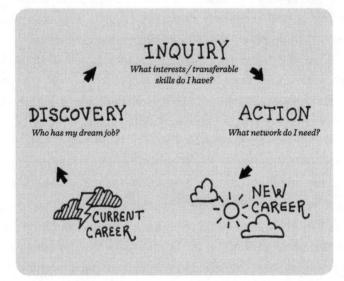

After a back-of-the-envelope assessment of my career interests, skill set, and strengths, I began the research-and-development process of discovering what possible roles were available for someone with my experience. My initial informational interviews came about after tapping into an existing network of friends in Toronto who had transitioned from legal careers to management roles (career networking reminder: stay on friendly terms with former coworkers) followed by seeking introductions through friends and friends of friends (career networking reminder: having a warm introduction will almost surely result in a productive conversation). Through this process, I was able to clarify the type of role and responsibility I was seeking before setting out on my next, more challenging networking goal: to build an entirely new network of professional contacts.

You see, once I knew exactly what role I wanted in the next stage of my legal career—a professional development role in a large New York City–based law firm—I realized that while my network was not exactly the wrong one to help me, it definitely was an incomplete one. And as these roles were being brought to the surface by word of mouth, I really needed an expanded network so I'd be top-of-mind when the next job opening occurred.

INQUIRY
LAWYER
∴ Existing Networks ∴
FINANCE   COLLEAGUES
BANKING   FRIENDS

Here's the networking reality check: that new community took me eighteen months to build! That's not a lifetime but not an insignificant amount of time either, especially when you're seeking a paycheck. In those months I was constantly meeting new people and gathering expertise in my desired field of employment. I attended conferences, joined committees, circulated articles to my new contacts, went on informational interviews, and relentlessly stayed in touch with everyone I was meeting. I purposefully connected and networked for the job I wanted.

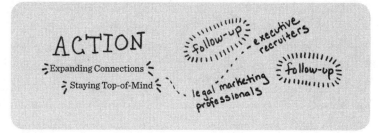

For me, that eighteen months was a wake-up call to not only maintain existing professional relationships but to grow connections before you ever think you'll need them.

One Size Fits None

I hate to have to remind you of this (again), but not all your networks or contacts will be suited to solving all your problems. To think a single network solves all problems is an error, even when you're not making a big career change! If I'd relied on a single network, in all likelihood I'd still be practicing law in Toronto. And if I'd continued to only grow my professional development network and skipped that 85 Broads networking breakfast, maybe I'd still be a manager of professional development or manager of alumni programs at a professional-services firm.

Daily, I slice and dice my network, reaching out to different contacts depending on the answer I'm seeking or problem I'm facing. When I had doubts about the strength of my writing, I turned to some of my mentors, whose words of encouragement spurred me to keep blogging. When a not-for-profit in the arts-in-education space asked me to join its benefit committee, I mailed out just five invitations to the event—as I knew five people in my network cared deeply about this issue. To mail any additional invitations would have been spam and a waste of stamps. In 2015 the connections I tapped to find a literary agent did not belong to the same group of contacts I regularly turn to for startup deal flow or speaking opportunities or introductions to journalists.

Different problems and goals need the brainpower of different connections. Avoid continuously seeking answers from the same core group of people. Good advice I received from a former tech executive is to always float new ideas by a group of people who don't necessarily share your viewpoint (let's hope you have some of those folks in your network!). The point is to ensure your network has all the tools and perspectives you need in it—and that you choose wisely when you tap your network for advice.

Networking is always about relationships, which means it is all about the information and experiences those particular relationships can bring to bear on your behalf. That's why I'll keep prodding you to pursue your goals by this process:

And once again, this is why you need to think about why you're reaching out to a particular person or group for help or guidance or direction—and about where your news, insights, and opportunities are coming from.

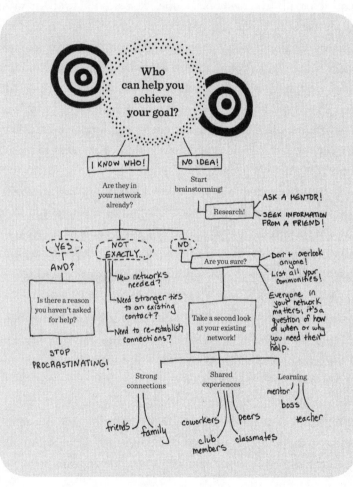

Expert Insights: Network Around the Corporation to Move Up the Ladder

You can't overlook the importance of making strong connections simply because you currently have a job. Networking is not just about landing the next job or promotion; it also plays a big part in how you get your job done today or if you'll meet your project deadline tomorrow. Supportive colleagues can help you get your job done faster and be a source of vital information for the next promotion or lateral career change.

My move from manager of professional development to manager of global alumni programs at White & Case was facilitated by the strong internal reputation I'd earned over four years at the firm and the even stronger relationships I'd established with colleagues across departments (as well as offices). I cannot say this enough: those relationships were absolutely essential as I was handed a challenging global role requiring massive creativity (as I had no staff and zero budget). You quickly find out what your reputation is and who has your back when the only way to do your job is to rely on collegiality and goodwill (plus calling in a few past favors).

Cultivating relationships up, down, and sideways on the corporate organization chart has always been a priority for me. And I imagined I was pretty good at it—that is, until I was introduced to Joe Styler. In 2005, Joe started at GoDaddy in a technical support role, and ten years later he's networked up, around, across, and down the corporate ladder to a coveted management position in the aftermarket department. For someone who landed an entry position at the company without having any experience other than assisting friends when they had computer problems, Joe's networked approach to career advancement within GoDaddy can be described as both generous and persistent. It's definitely an example worth following.

Q: You've been at GoDaddy for over ten years, working your way up from the call center in a very focused and networked way. How did you approach finding new opportunities within the company?

Joe: I first figured out how to do my current job really well, and doing that opened the doors to other opportunities. My first role was in sales and I really couldn't sell well—so I looked for the top salesperson in the company and sought his advice. I used to sit next to him regularly and listen to what he did on sales calls (this meant coming in early before my shift as well as on days off until I was able to get the hang of selling).

Being prepared to seek help and mentoring from others within the company, as well as investing in my own professional development, has been invaluable not only for advancing my career but also in how I get my job done day-to-day. I have advocates across the company in various departments and function areas. I have numerous trusted relationships and mentors I can seek advice from.

Q: You became intrigued by the aftermarket aspect of the domain business, an area of the industry you initially knew nothing about. How did you approach this challenge? What steps did you take to become an expert in this area?

Joe: Aftermarket is a highly competitive department to get into and positions rarely open up. I understood that I had to become an expert in this area of the business to even be considered for a role, as getting up to speed once I landed a role was not an option in this competitive area of the domain industry! I also knew I would have to get to know the people working in the department in order to discover if there were possible job openings. Again, I approached the challenge by investing my personal time in learning the role, by meeting with members of the team, then following up on their advice. Rather than communicating over e-mail or via instant message, I invested my personal time to meet with them face-to-face. Developing those personal relationships was key.

Q: It took some time before there was an opening with the aftermarket group. Describe how you stayed top-of-mind with the decision makers.

Joe: From start to job offer, it took approximately two years to get a position in the aftermarket department.

I made sure every month I spent some time with the people in the department in person. I always followed up on advice or suggestions they gave me. I routinely checked in with the vice president overseeing the department. This guy traveled frequently, so continually staying in touch with the other employees in the department really helped, as they would let me know every few weeks when the VP was going to be back in the office!

A hopeful sign that I could be considered for a role came a year into my networking efforts: the VP invited me to dinner with the entire aftermarket team. I still remember how excited I was, and calling my wife to let her know I would be home late that night. It was still several months before I was offered a role, but I was encouraged to continue my efforts after that dinner.

Q: Were you ever discouraged or deterred from your networking efforts as you pursued a role in this particular department? How did you manage that?

Joe: There were many times I was discouraged because an opportunity did not appear overnight (irrational, because I was fully aware from the start that positions rarely opened up in aftermarket). My tactic to get back on track was to focus on the things I could control—that is, I continued to focus on improving my skills for the role I was in and mentoring others.

Q: You're a powerful observer of human interactions and business needs. How has that factored in your professional success?

Joe: Just as my career has advanced with the help of others, I make it my job to help those reporting to me grow in their current positions or advance into other roles within the company. This has been invaluable. I have always tried to help others improve and achieve things they dreamed of, which meant many times losing some of my top performers to other teams or departments. On the flip side, this approach has resulted in having a lot of friends and strong advocates across the company.

Q: Looking outside of GoDaddy, you have a deep, industry-focused network and are acknowledged within the industry for your expertise. How have you gone about establishing your reputation and network? Why did you see the need to have connections and visibility across the industry?

Joe: Just like landing the position in the aftermarket department, my industry connections are not something that just happened overnight or as a result of a first meeting or attending a single conference. I have consistently put myself out there (which is challenging, as I am an introvert). It shouldn't come as a surprise, but I always research the new people I'm meeting.

Increasingly, I see the importance of networking as part of a team—that is, the formal and informal groups we all can choose to be a part of. You can choose to simply show up at work every day, or you can actively engage with your colleagues. The more visible and trusted you are in your industry, the more ability you have to leverage the strengths and expertise of others when you're pursuing something new. It also makes you more productive (and we all know our time is as valuable as our relationships)!

Yes, You Do Have a Network

Networking always starts with who you already know: those key connections, groups, or communities with whom you interact regularly. People who know you, like you, and trust you—and if asked, will help you. People you've shared experiences with.

If your first knee-jerk reaction is "But, I don't know anyone!" pause for a second and give your network a little more thought.

Question: What is LinkedIn?

It's a contact list! It's job-search information! It's a media channel! It's a social platform that assumes you know someone before you are even allowed to connect with him or her! It's all of the above!

I'm a big fan of LinkedIn, for its functionality as a contact-management platform and as an instructional tool on the ins and outs of networking.

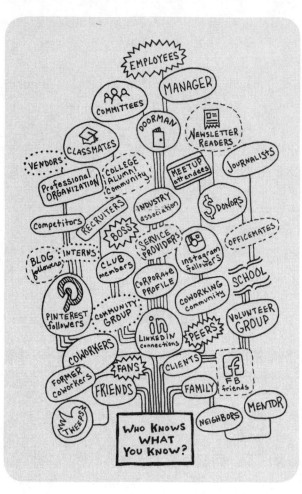

LinkedIn requires you to have some sort of preexisting relationship with someone before you can connect. Knowing someone directly or seeking an introduction to someone via a trusted mutual connection has always been the strongest way to network when you're seeking help. Don't let technology fool you into thinking any differently.

LinkedIn is also invaluable in expanding networks—not only revealing those indirect second- and third-degree connections, but also in showing us who we share experiences with. Experiences, such as shared employers or schools or internships or community service, create connections. These are the touchpoints for creating stronger bonds. The shared experience of having attended the same college or summer camp or having worked for the same employer spark further interest and deeper engaged conversation. Okay, it may also be that misery (or miserable experiences) loves to connect, which is not necessarily a bad thing when you're striking up a conversation with someone for the first time.

The point is, your network is bigger than your first-degree connections (such as your college BFF or the group you regularly sit next to in your coworking space). And LinkedIn has been largely responsible for educating millions of people about this.

Think back to all of the bits of information Jessica Peltz-Zatulove had to hunt for, online and off, then meticulously write down in a notebook during her job search in 2002. Much of it (and so much more) is now readily accessible on LinkedIn and other social platforms. More data in one place does not diminish the need for a thoroughly researched networking effort—it simply means your ability to source valuable bits of networking information is accelerated.

Expert Insights: Tap into Your Crowd for Success

Raising money is one of those rather ambitious goals that has been democratized as a result of the Internet and the proliferation of crowdfunding platforms. In 2014, $16.2 billion was raised on these platforms, up from $6.1 billion in 2013, and in 2015 the amounts raised exceeded $34 billion globally.[16]

Crowdfunding platforms, however, are useless in the absence of a project sponsor with a strong existing network to tap into and decent community-coordination skills. Because here's the crowdfunding reality: most campaigns fail! Only about 45 percent of crowdfunding campaigns ever successfully reach their funding goals (and 14 percent of projects fail to raise any money at all).[17] Crowdfunding is not the answer to your lack of funding woes; networking is.

To confirm or dispel my notions about the utility of crowdfunding platforms, I reached out to entrepreneur Kathryn Finney. Kathryn is the founder and managing director of digitalundivided, a social enterprise that invests in the success of black and Latina women tech founders and operates the BIG Innovation Center in Atlanta, Georgia. She's also an author, blogger, and former editor-at-large for *BlogHer*; and in 2015 she successfully conducted a crowdfunding campaign on the Kickstarter platform.

Q: You've had a number of successful ventures, including the launch of digitalundivided and subsequent sale of *Budget Fashionista*. Why did you decide to crowdfund your current project, a first for you? Why was the time right to turn to your community for financial support?

Kathryn: A little background to set the story. My current venture is a social enterprise with three primary components:

- digitalundivided has supported black women tech entrepreneurs since 2012 through a highly successful accelerator/incubator program (FOCUS Fellows). Top tech organizations such as Google, Microsoft, Facebook, and Etsy have partnered with us in this effort.

- #ProjectDiane is a data-collection project to share details on black women startup founders. It was launched in early 2015 to support (with data) the digitalundivided programming.
- *#ReWriteTheCode* is a documentary exploring the intersection of race and gender in technology. The documentary is the final phase of #ProjectDiane.

I had collaborators and partners—as this was a community effort, after all—and we knew that it would be very hard to communicate the value of the *#ReWriteTheCode* documentary to the tech and startup community—let alone seek funding through traditional investor channels! However, we knew our community wanted the *#ReWriteTheCode* story to be told, and we needed money to make it happen, so we leaned on our existing connections and launched a crowdfunding campaign.

Q: Describe how you approached the campaign. Why were you so successful when so many crowdfunding efforts fail?

Kathryn: We spent about a month planning the details of the campaign, but the reason it became so successful is that it was grounded in a network I had already built.

In 2003, I started as one of the very first lifestyle bloggers on the web. Eventually, I branched out to print and TV, including a stint as a correspondent for the *TODAY* show. A whole generation of now very powerful women grew up reading my blog. These connections and experiences paved the way for my next venture, digitalundivided.

Since launching in 2012, digitalundivided has coalesced into a network. We've engaged thousands of people through newsletters, events, and programming (like FOCUS Fellows). As a result, we had a vibrant, strong existing community to leverage prior to the launch of the crowdfunding campaign. A solid reputation after years of really delivering on promises helps too!

As to the actual crowdfunding campaign, our success can be summed up as this: ask early and ask often!

A month prior to campaign kickoff, we reached out to all our friends and shared our campaign goals with them. That's how we got a large number of backers and broke our target goal of $25,000 in the first forty-eight hours of the campaign. Throughout the entire thirty-day campaign, we consistently tweeted out to other potential supporters and kept our supporters in the loop: regular e-mail updates on funding goals, the multiple ways they could help us achieve the next funding milestone, etc. Ongoing communications helped the digitalundivided community "own" the process of making the campaign a success (which in turn encouraged them to support us more). The community really amplified our efforts as they rallied their friends and followers to become part of *#ReWriteTheCode*.

Q: What did you learn personally and professionally from your crowdfunding effort?

Kathryn: The strength of your personal network is one of the biggest deciding factors for success of crowdfunding campaigns (especially service-based ones). People are investing, donating, and pledging because they believe in *you*, and in return you have to give them a reason to believe. Over 30 percent of our backers came from the digitalundivided team's personal network. We tapped *every* network we have or have been part of: alumni associations, clubs and sports teams, friends, family, and, yes, even ex-boyfriends.

It is important to open up and ask for help. I discovered that people *do* want to help, but you have to give them the opportunity (and ways) to help. Keep in mind that most of the world is pretty busy and won't know you need help unless you ask for it.

Q: Generosity is an important networking concept. How did it play out in your crowdfunding efforts?

Kathryn: I'm a believer in the idea of "return on generosity." If you don't have a network of people you think you can really turn to for help, then you probably have a super-low return on generosity. What is the reason for someone investing in your project if you've never made similar investments of time, money, or other resources in other people, projects, or things? The most frequent reason we heard as to why people backed *#ReWriteTheCode* was our track record of giving back combined with making our network feel good about giving and becoming part of a bigger project.

Q: What indicators did you have before you launched your campaign that your community was willing to support you?

Kathryn: I remember a dear friend asked me the same question a few days before the end of campaign. I told her, "To be perfectly honest, I really didn't know if we could do it." However, what I did know was digitalundivided did great work supporting urban tech entrepreneurs, and as with all my entrepreneurial ventures, I had built a strong network.

And we did our due diligence prior to launching the campaign. A month before our campaign kickoff, we sent a segmented e-mail outreach for the project—to people in our network who we believed would back us financially or champion the campaign or perhaps do both—and we received tremendous feedback that helped us understand what financial goals to set for *#ReWriteTheCode* (plus who in our network we could truly rely upon to write a check or amplify our message).

Q: How did you mitigate failure? What were the risks you associated with being unsuccessful in your crowdfunding efforts?

Kathryn: The best way to mitigate failure is to build your community. Having a ton of Facebook or Twitter followers/fan doesn't make an active community. A mistake I've observed in other crowdfunding campaigns is an overreliance on a large social media following and foolishly assuming this will somehow convert into a donating, engaged, and participatory community. What works is direct engagement with people who really know you—then sending those folks a lot of personalized communications or direct messages, or go old-school targeted e-mail or even phone calls. Don't kid yourself into thinking the platform will do the work for you!

We also mitigated failure by setting a very conservative goal of $25,000 to produce a fifteen-minute film—as we were sure our community could rally to raise that targeted amount. The crowdfunding platform simply facilitated the processing of payments from the community. We did set stretch fund-raising goals because we really wanted to create a longer film, and ultimately we raised over $59,000 from 702 donors.

Stop Googling and Start Observing

We have become a Google generation (or Bing, Yahoo, Baidu—pick your search engine of choice). The problem is that we cast out a question, seeking an immediate and simple answer, rather than getting curious and researching the bigger context.

It is a side product of the instant, mobile, and real-time world we engage in—and not a good side product at that, as it is a networking headache.

In real-life engagements, this kind of searching has replaced curiosity and intellectual rigor. When we search online, we scan the first screen page and grab a suitable answer. Here's where that googling habit goes afoul IRL: there is tendency to simply ask rather than *inquire* before asking. When you constantly use your networks like a search engine, one of two things is likely to happen:

- You won't get the answer you're looking for, or
- You won't get any answer at all

Reread Jessica Peltz-Zatulove's job-search story: it is an excellent example of how powerful networking results are attained when you start by observing. As Jessica indicates, the only difference in the networking process today (and when she was hunting for a job) is where you'll find the information you need to ignite your research toward your goal.

You can't expect your network to do all the networking for you. Social networking sites, blogs, online media sites, and wikis have provided us with a wealth of valuable information, more than enough to the answer the questions we have—the real challenge now is to embark on a Q&A path that is more about discovery, and a little less about expediency, before we turn to our networks for help.

Invest the time—not only will your connections thank you, they'll invest more time in helping you reach your goal too.

Know Your Audience

"If you think of anyone . . ."

I get asked big, open-ended questions like this frequently, and it's most frustrating when the question is posed by a change-the-world type (aka tech entrepreneurs who are generally regarded as sharp innovators, having spent time and energy researching, designing, and releasing tech products into the world). The discipline, rigor, and curiosity they apply to the problem they are solving completely vaporizes when they arrive at researching the connections their startup needs to take an idea or product forward. They simply demand an answer to the one vital question they have, long before they start asking for an introduction.

From where I sit as an investor in the startup world, researching potential investors involves having a personality that is part investment analyst and part archaeologist, part stalker and part paparazzi, and that is also a huge dose of private investigator. It means discovering the person behind that "investor" title—who are they, how they think, what teams they invest in—not simply speculating on the size of the check the startup wants (or needs) the investor to write.

I use the example of tech entrepreneurs because it is such an obvious one—but the same rigor should be applied when you ask any of your connections for help. The more you understand how someone can *specifically* help you, the more they will be able to do so. That passion you've tapped to build your business or to reimagine your career path—well, dedicate the same level of relentless curiosity to researching the connections you need to take your idea forward.

Understand Your Audience

My career started before mobile and corporate intranets. Work was done at the office or lugged home in a briefcase to be continued well into the night at the kitchen table. A lot of time was spent in the actual office because that's where all the resources necessary to do the job were. How times have changed—except that we still work with and alongside other people. Knowing how to connect well with others remains a key piece of our career-success puzzle. If we could just look beyond our deadlines and the need for expedited answers and engage with our colleagues!

Let me give you an example from 1993 that still has relevance today.

John Chapman is a litigation partner at the Canadian firm Miller Thomson (as mentioned, I started my career at the firm's office in Toronto). A smart attorney with a wicked sense of humor, John used to "grade" the memos or briefs I drafted for his review, in red pen, like a law school professor. "I gave you a B plus this time," he'd say with a laugh before detailing the ways I could improve my work. He was a terrific mentor, and from his peculiar tactics I managed to learn quite a bit (ensuring I would not want to become a litigator, ever).

It concerned me to discover that other associates didn't feel the same admiration for John or that working for him was a positive learning experience. In the midst of yet another story about what a jerk of a partner he was, I interrupted to ask a simple question:

"What time of day do you go to speak with John about your project or research?"

The young attorney's answer was "Sometime in mid to late afternoon."

I shook my head. Fatal mistake. John *was* a complete jerk to deal with after lunch. You see, at the time John was the father of young children, and he liked to have dinner with his family at home each night and help put the kids to bed before diving back into client work. Recall that in those days there were no mobile devices or web portals (let alone Skype), so every night John had to drag home a large barrister's briefcase full of papers. His afternoons at the office were spent powering through as much work as humanly possible before packing up what remained for that day and catching a five thirty train. John structured his workday around his personal life, and these associates had failed to pick up on his cues.

Before noon, John allowed time to mentor and advise. After lunch, he was highly focused, so inquiries from associates were received as unwanted interruptions. As soon as my colleagues learned this about him and switched to scheduling meetings, not at times that were convenient for them, but in the morning when it was optimal for him, their experience of working with him completely shifted too.

Of course, I'm now pondering what grade John would give this networking advice.

Expert Insights: Who Should Know, Like, and Trust You

The key takeaway for you right now is to network to build strong relationships and do it long before you ever think you'll need them! Alison Levine understands this better than anyone I know.

Alison operates in extreme environments. She's an adventurer, plus a best-selling author and a sought-after speaker on leadership. Oh, and she's made history (twice) as team captain of the first American Women's Everest Expedition and then as the first American to complete a six-hundred-mile traverse from western Antarctica to the South Pole. A member of the Adventurers Grand Slam club (you only get invited to join that exclusive network once you've climbed the highest peak on each continent and skied to both poles), Alison knows it is a life-or-death necessity to create strong personal bonds within a community in order to reach your goals—really!

Q: In chapter 4 of your book *On the Edge: Leadership Lessons from Mount Everest and Other Extreme Environments*[18] you tell readers, "You reduce your chances of being passed by when you have strong relationships in place." As an adventurer and explorer, having an extended network is a strategic decision. Describe how you go about making those essential relationships in situations where everyone you're meeting is aiming for the same goal.

Alison: First thing I do when I get to base camp on any mountain is walk around and talk to every other team that's there. People think I am doing this because I am extremely social, but that's not why I make the rounds (I'm an introvert, by the way). I want to get to know people on other teams because if anything should happen to one of my team members high up on one of these mountains, I want the people around us to feel a connection and an obligation to help us. It is a very strategic decision.

There are a lot of factors that go into whether or not someone can be rescued from high up on the mountain, but one thing that always works in people's favor is knowing the people who are heading up the route at the same time. Because people who know you are more likely to go out of their way for you and perhaps to take on a large amount of personal risk on your behalf.

Q: In your book you also introduce the concept of the networked leader. Many of us have that one highly connected go-to person in our personal networks. However, in the case of mountaineers, you note that the best-networked leaders aren't always climbing alongside their team and you warn against relying on a single connection to pull you through a difficult situation. Can you discuss this a little more?

Alison: Well, if you saw the movie *Everest*, you'll be familiar with the 1996 Mount Everest disaster where two of the world's best, most experienced high-altitude mountain guides became separated from their teams during their summit bid. As the climbers were descending, they were caught in a ferocious storm. Because those two leaders were not around to guide their respective teams back down to their tents, the climbers were unable to get back to camp safely. I'm simplifying the story here of course (and there were other factors that came into play as well), but this is an extreme example of how things can go horribly wrong if you rely on only one person to get you through a difficult situation.

Q: Corporate sponsorship was essential to making the first American Women's Everest Expedition a reality. Talk about how you connected the dots from seeing a Ford Expedition on display at a farmer's market to figuring out that a business school contact was employed at Ford.

Alison: Well, I had been racking my brain trying to come up with ideas for sponsors for our trip. I had sent letters (this was

2002, so people still used snail mail) and e-mails to all the obvious choices—gear companies, sporting goods companies, outdoor apparel companies—and wasn't having much luck. I was getting burned out and discouraged. I finally decided to take a break from all things Everest and treat myself to an afternoon of fun at the Half Moon Bay Art & Pumpkin Festival. It was there that I happened across a concept car from Ford that was on display—the Himalaya Expedition! Seeing the concept car was a lightbulb moment: I could approach Ford to sponsor the expedition!

My MBA class at Duke was pretty small, around three hundred people, so I knew where most of my classmates were working (which was a good thing, as LinkedIn did not yet exist). I reached out to a classmate, Kevin Ropp, who worked for Ford. He was working in the Mercury division in Southern California, so while he wasn't down the hall from the CEO's office in Dearborn, Michigan, Kevin was able to help me successfully funnel the idea of sponsoring the Everest expedition up the internal corporate channels to the right people at Ford. The rest is history.

Q: You have a large, diverse network from Wall Street to the seven summits. How do you manage to stay connected with them all?

Alison: I don't really take phone calls anymore. I only use e-mail. I can knock out e-mails at 2:00 a.m. or when I am on planes. E-mail communication allows me to be more efficient. Everyone says, "I just need ten minutes of your time." Well, I am only home a few days a month, and I want that time to be quality time with my loved ones. If I gave everyone who asked just ten minutes of my time, my entire day would be gone every day of the week. With e-mail I can communicate when it works for me. I also have friends all over the world in all different time zones, so e-mail is such an easy way to stay connected.

Q: Any additional guidance you have for others who are tapping into their personal networks to solve an identified business need?

Alison: Do your homework before you approach people for a big ask. Find out what is important to them. If you cannot take the time to google someone and scour their website and their social media feeds to gather as much information as you can about them before approaching them for help, then they shouldn't waste their time helping you.

The Power of Small Actions

We can all make time for a little networking in our hyper-focused lives; all it takes is some thought about who we're connecting with, combined with some strategy.

Do you have two minutes during your weekday morning to post an update on LinkedIn? That update could be a cross-selling opportunity for your business. Using the stairs or public transport might take you slightly out of your way, but what if you see that detour, not as a decision about transportation but as an opportunity for a valuable interaction? For example, if a startup founding team had shifted their mind-set on how to get from point A to point B, they might have found that taking the subway instead of a cab would have meant extending their conversation with an investor by twenty absolutely invaluable minutes.

Sometimes you miss a networking beat by not taking time to consider the golden connection that's right in front of you.

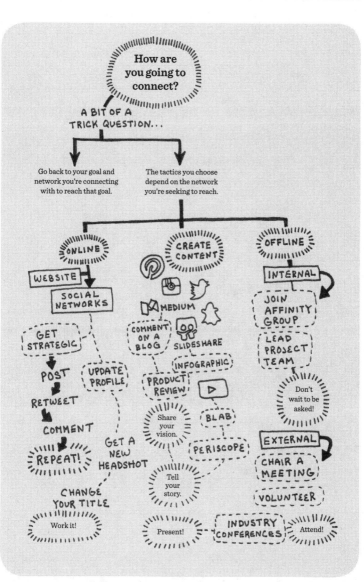

A small networking challenge to try: grab coffee with a colleague or pick a different seat in the coworking space tomorrow, and see what happens.

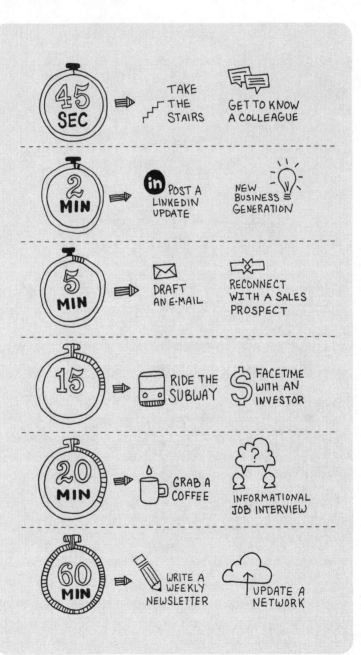

Open Your Own Doors

You've already read Joe Styler's and Jessica Peltz-Zatulove's stories. What's interesting to me is that their deliberate and focused efforts to create the career opportunities they were seeking very much mirror the efforts 85 Broads founder Janet Hanson took to land her jobs at Goldman Sachs—thirty years ago.

Here is what is also interesting (and slightly unusual) about Janet's career at Goldman Sachs: she was in and out of the venerable investment banking firm four times—yes, four times! And because of that "out of building" experience, Janet started 85 Broads. But let's not jump ahead to 85 Broads just yet. Janet's forays in and out of the same firm, each time returning in a very different role and to a different functional area, is yet another networking lesson in creating opportunities for yourself.

Janet first stepped into Goldman Sachs while attending Columbia Business School. An "opportunity semester" in fixed-income research provided her with four or so months to network around the investment bank (the firm only occupied a mere five floors back then). Allowed to wander, Janet spent time researching the different divisions, rather than simply becoming an expert on fixed income, and discovered her interest in bond markets in the process. Knowing that to have any chance of landing a job on the trading floor she'd have to speak the language of sales and trading, Janet set to work becoming an expert in that area. When she found out the guys on the trading floor held regular training sessions and meetings, she pleaded to be allowed to attend.

An internship at Goldman Sachs was just an internship, not necessarily a stepping-stone to a career (or a fast track to bypass the typical ten to twelve interviews for a full-time job at the firm). However, networking changed the outcome for Janet. By understanding the business and sharing a common language with her interviewers, Janet connected quickly with decision makers and, after the internship ended, landed a job on the trading floor.

Throughout the career that followed, Janet kept returning because she recognized that she needed to be in the firm, surrounded by really smart, driven people. That sense of purpose (together with awareness of what fulfilled her professionally) paved the way for her career trajectory. Each time she returned to the company it was in a different role. Being curious, taking a high interest in learning and understanding what your colleagues in the workplace do each day, is a factor Janet credits in helping her continually reinvent her career within Goldman Sachs. That career reinvention was not frictionless. Janet stresses the ability to put ego aside to try something new as essential for success.

Everyone's an Expert

Back in chapter 1, I shared four truths about this hyperconnected work era:

- Everyone is an expert
- College degrees can be bypassed
- Anyone can start a company—anywhere
- Meritocracy is BS

We can lay claim to our careers and call ourselves anything in the process (and on our business cards). That's the massive upside, if and when we choose to take control of what it is we want to achieve. Because, as I've also said earlier in this book, at a time when connections make the difference between landing the next gig or staying in your current job, it's not a question of what you know or who you know but rather *who knows what you know* that tips the balance.

What sets you apart? For me, it's my knack of seeing the connections among ideas, people, and opportunities. I'm wired to connect the networking dots. But even I didn't see the bigger opportunity (and lay claim to my expertise) until 2013, when some self-proclaimed networking experts started tapping into my ideas for their projects and presentations. That told me it was time to proactively claim my expertise in blogs, on panels, in my bio, and anywhere else I could think of! Time to not merely nod politely when someone acknowledged my superconnector status but to give my network the content to prove it and the links to share it.

The Three Ps

What makes networking efforts successful? People! People! People! Even the most digitally savvy networkers understand this. That's part of the reason why tactics are the final element of my networking equation:

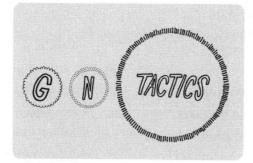

Tactics are meant to reinforce the human element of the networking equation. It's the choice you make between picking up the phone, sending a card, or posting a message on someone's birthday. What's the best way to reach that other person? Admit it: there are people in your current network whose e-mails you ignore, tweets you mute, and Facebook posts you've stopped following because you just don't get what they are saying. Perhaps they're socially awkward or perhaps they're focusing too much on the platform and not spending enough time thinking about whom they are communicating with (and why).

My message is simple: design your networking strategy around people, not platforms! But don't rush into joining a networking group or spend hours online pinning or posting before you've figured out which connections you're tapping into and/or the relationships you're looking to strengthen. The tactics you select need to support your goal by connecting you in the most effective way to the people you've identified in your network who can help you achieve your goal.

In other words, don't commit yet another random act of networking by taking steps to connect before you've given consideration to whom you really need to connect with. The tactic(s) you choose should be the best methods to reach them.

Networking Is Never Finished

At any stage of your career, a new opportunity requires building a new network or reworking existing connections in a new way—simply relying on your current networking status quo is not enough. In 2011, I knocked on a lot of venture-capital, angel-investor, and startup doors to discuss the Women Innovate Mobile accelerator concept. Many doors were opened for me on the basis of reputation—mine, that of my cofounders, and, most important, that of our contacts, who initiated many introductions. What I was doing in 2011 was replicating the networking process I had undertaken in 2002 to change careers, this time aided by additional social networking tactics such as LinkedIn and Twitter.

And in preparing to write this book, I had to do it all over again.

4

Clubs, Crowds, Committees, and Cohorts

You can't turn a corner or post a status update without running into an "exclusive" this or "must-join" group for that. The opportunities to connect with others by participating on a committee or as part of a club or mastermind group have proliferated like Starbucks locations.

I joined the global business-networking group 85 Broads (now known as Ellevate) in early 2009, after years of being hounded by a friend who happened to be a longtime member of the group as well as a former employee of Goldman Sachs, the Wall Street investment-banking firm that inspired the formation of 85 Broads. Frankly, I hadn't grasped the value of being a member and I believed, in an accurate but narrow way, that I already had a sufficient number of networking options before me. I was on several committees at work, engaged in the relevant industry associations and conferences for the profession I was in, and was vice-chair of a New York City–based not-for-profit board.

Didn't I have enough networking on my plate? What additional group networking could I possibly need?

You have already heard where my story with 85 Broads ends. But where it truly started was at the first breakfast meeting I attended after joining. After years of being prodded by my friend Marla, I'd relented. I'd completed my online profile and signed up to attend an upcoming Power Breakfast organized by the New York chapter at a midtown restaurant not far from my office. I cannot recall who the speaker was, but this I do know: I showed up alone at the appointed time (early!) with my business cards in hand. Sitting down at a table with complete strangers, I really had no idea what to expect. And, remember, I don't particularly enjoy walking into a roomful of strangers.

I was blown away. Conversation flowed comfortably. Introductions and contact information were freely exchanged. And I'm sure the speaker suitably inspired—as I know I put the date for the next Power Breakfast in my calendar immediately. And before I left the event, I had introduced myself to the organizers and 85 Broads' staff and offered to assist at a future event.

As entrepreneur and chief strategy officer of House of Genius, Jonathan Beninson explains how he decides whether to join a networking group: "If it is not 'Heck yes!' then it's no. Trust your gut."

Well, 85 Broads was a "heck yes" networking group for me.

It's Voluntary

With the exception of insane asylums and prisons, most communities are voluntary.

Attending a college reunion or paying your alumni-association dues (or engaging in any of a lengthy list of possible examples of group interaction) is a voluntary act, entirely dependent on the value you perceive you will get in exchange for your participation. I truly had no expectations when I attended my first 85 Broads event. Based on word-of-mouth recommendations, I knew the organization had a strong reputation and that was enough to get me to sign up for a Power Breakfast—once. As for going back, well, that's another matter altogether. The decision to continue to attend events and to willingly pay an annual membership fee was based entirely on the value I received.

When participation is voluntary, you can get really involved or you can walk out the door at any time. Community is all about individual interactions within a group effort.

With no shortage of groups to join, disengaging is expected, and signing on to something new occurs with rapid, click-through ease. Deciding to be part of something takes about the same effort as unfriending someone on Facebook. We're fickle as a flash mob in our interests (and thanks to our obsession with our smartphones, our attention spans are now shorter than a goldfish's—yes, Microsoft conducted a study to prove this). All of this makes it challenging for organizers to continually get community engagement, member interaction, and network communications just right, ensuring that members will regularly show up. Grab our attention, provide us with high value, or—guess what? We'll go elsewhere.

But how you choose to engage once you've decided to join the club is also voluntary.

My 85 Broads experience was different from that of most members because I *chose* to get involved. I voluntarily gave the organization a lot of my time, well before I became its president. By volunteering and spending time with Janet Hanson and her staff in order to better understand how I could contribute to the network, my involvement stretched beyond the typical membership level—as did the valuable benefits I received in return from the network. I didn't simply check the membership box and show up expecting to be entertained. I asked questions, I observed, and I interacted beyond the expected membership parameters.

Joining is voluntary and so is choosing how you will participate. Daily, on multiple platforms and in many networking venues, you get to make the same choice.

A Platform and a Purpose

Back in the nineties, maintaining relationships with successful former employees was not a priority on Wall Street. Blame it on the firm culture that was pervasive then or the expectation of being a "lifer" when it came to employment—whatever the explanation, corporate alumni or "returnship" initiatives were not the norm.

Janet Hanson saw this as an opportunity. And in 1997 she launched 85 Broads. It started simply enough: dinner at the Water Club, as a way for a group of women who had previously worked at Goldman Sachs headquarters in New York City to gather, reconnect, and reminisce. A nice evening—but Janet knew at dinner that a "glory days" alumni-focused effort was not going to take off and result in something bigger and more meaningful.

Then along came the Internet.

Two years after the original dinner gathering, Janet "dot-com'd" the network, and that changed everything. With a global online platform, there was now a way to connect between cocktails and canapés. Geographic boundaries were eliminated, so alums who were no longer in New York City could participate too. From a one-off social gathering arose a transformative powerhouse business network.

What made 85 Broads so powerful? You can't discount an incredibly visionary leader who was among the first to create an online social platform for members; however, these additional factors made the network truly dynamic:

- It was composed of highly motivated members who made a conscious decision to opt in. Members made a commitment to be part of the network, and that led to a remarkable level of engagement.
- Members enthusiastically brought their expertise and new relationships to the network for the benefit of other members.
- Members shared values and spoke a common language (business). There was a respect for what every member had done to get ahead professionally, which in turn created a high level of trust among the members.

85 Broads was also focused. As a networking platform, it existed for one reason: to solve problems for its members, be it funding or a board position or guidance on how to get promoted. It was not trying to be all things to anyone seeking to connect with a former Wall Street executive for social interaction or networking opportunities.

Expert Insights: Pursue Your Passion

Getting to know other people and breaking through the awkwardness of initial introductions is always easier when the connections are made with shared purpose or interest. For novelist

Aidan Donnelley Rowley, it is her massive love of books—not simply writing them but the bigger joy that comes from sharing her passion for reading with others. Back when her first book, *Life After Yes*,[19] was on the verge of hitting the bookshelves, Aidan launched Happier Hours,[20] a modern literary salon. I remember the very first event: Aidan's apartment was absolutely jammed with enthusiastic book lovers who were delighted to discover fellow members of their tribe. Aidan's passion for books, and not the guarantee of a packed event, is the engine that drives Happier Hours. Networking tip: undertake your own community-building efforts because you care really deeply about the subject matter or topic, not with the aim of a definite outcome or result.

Q: When did you launch Happier Hours? Who attends?

Aidan: I launched Happier Hours in March 2009. My guests are a diverse group of women in a broad range of careers. I would say that their one commonality is that they love books and love to connect over books and the conversations they inspire.

Q: Why did you launch Happier Hours, and what's happened since then?

Aidan: When I originally launched Happier Hours I was anticipating the publication of my first novel, and I began hosting the events as a means of meeting and communing with fellow writers and creative people in the New York City area. Also, I missed the deep, edifying discussions about books and ideas that were common in my college and law-school days but not as much in my new life as a young mother. Since its inception, Happier Hours has evolved in wonderful ways I could never have predicted. Today, these evenings are all about interesting and interested women connecting face-to-face, in an increasingly digital world, about great books and meaningful topics.

Q: Who are the members of the Happier Hours community? Can you describe a "typical" attendee of this modern literary salon?

Aidan: What I love, and celebrate, is that there is really no "typical" attendee. Certainly, there are many members of the publishing community—writers and editors and agents and publicists—but there is also a broad, eccentric range of attendees, from fellow mothers at my girls' schools to producers of Broadway plays to news anchors and banking titans. There are no rules at all about who should come, and who does, and this is what makes these nights so vibrant and unique.

Q: Happier Hours is now in New York City and in LA. Was there a plan behind this expansion to the West Coast?

Aidan: There was no formal plan to expand Happier Hours to the West Coast; the growth was wonderfully organic. I hosted my friend, and author, Claire Bidwell Smith here in New York City for her memoir *The Rules of Inheritance*. After our event, she raved about the experience and said she wished there were such events in Los Angeles. And a seed was planted. Claire hosts out there, along with author Jillian Lauren and, more recently, Jenny Feldon as well.

Q: Happier Hours now has a website. Why did you feel that was the logical next step for this community?

Aidan: I was hesitant to build a site because these events have historically been so private and quirky, but as they have grown, it's been important to have a place that houses all information about the events.

Q: Any community-building guidance for others who may have a similar goal of bringing a niche group together over a common interest?

Aidan: I would say to start from a place of curiosity and passion. Though I harbored goals of meeting fellow authors and book lovers, my real starting point with Happier Hours was a personal longing for rich conversation around books. Quite simply, I wanted to host an event that I'd like to attend. It was obviously heartening to learn that there was such an appetite for this kind of gathering, and I was thrilled to build on this knowledge, but the idea was born from a place of interest, with no real agenda.

Q: Generosity is an important networking concept. How did it play out in the Happier Hours community?

Aidan: Generosity is everything. I love shining a light on authors and books I love. To me, this feels like a meaningful thing to do, and I've been doing this for many years and it's brought so much joy to my life. A wonderful result: the growth of an incredible community of thoughtful, kind, smart women.

Expert Insights: A Network for Today but Not Tomorrow

Varelie Croes and I were first officially introduced via e-mail. I recall it was one of those "you two should know each other" exchanges (which typically drive me nuts) and one of the very few that actually got it really, really right.

Varelie and I share a similar career path: law school to

scrambling up the corporate ladder then leaping right before reaching the top rung. We also recognized that having new and expanded networks of contacts was essential to achieving the next step in our professional lives. The networks we had at one point in time, so essential for propelling our legal careers forward (and navigating office politics or bonus negotiations), were not as helpful at the moment our career focus turned outward to new professional horizons.

Joining the global networking group 85 Broads (both as a member and then as its first president) was instrumental in transforming my career trajectory. For Varelie, it was recognizing that she needed a community of entrepreneurial-focused connections to guide her—then finding the right group to fill that void.

Q: Why did you decide to join a mastermind group?

Varelie: My core network of friends at the time were all executives and people in the financial, professional services, and legal industries. The vast majority were less than enthusiastic about their jobs but not willing to make a career change. As I began to think about changing my career future, I realized I needed connections in different industries who were enthusiastic about their career choices. It also was hard to change directions professionally without a support network to call upon when I was feeling lost. I knew I had to find a new core group who were facing challenges similar to mine. I'm also a crazy researcher, so I was overwhelmed by the amount of information out there on starting a business, rebranding, creating an online presence—and I quickly realized I would save a lot of time if I leveraged what other people had already done!

Q: Had you belonged to or joined other groups before?

Varelie: I was at PwC for eleven years, so my networks (internally and externally) were quite narrowly focused around my subject-matter expertise (tax and alternative investments). My networking really was limited to corporate groups and professional organizations, plus PwC's women's leadership network.

Q: What information or support did you feel you needed from a group like this that you couldn't otherwise get from your existing network?

Varelie: Definitely the diversity of the individuals in the group made for interesting conversation and brainstorming. I was able to see "me" and my ideas through many different lenses. The women in the mastermind group I selected all had different backgrounds and were ambitious entrepreneurs with big dreams. It was refreshing to get candid feedback on my ideas and projects, as opposed to when you go to your close friends and family who are naturally inclined to be supportive. Don't get me wrong—I needed that support too, but more than cheerleaders I needed candid feedback and help navigating the startup ecosystem.

Q: How did you go about discovering and selecting the group you joined?

Varelie: I attended digital entrepreneur Nathalie Lussier's Off the Charts event in New York City and casually over lunch met some incredible women who were applying for Nathalie's mastermind group. I vividly remember thinking: if this is the caliber of people who will join the mastermind group, I want to be a part of it. Connecting with those women made the decision easy. It was a big investment to participate, and while I probably could have figured it all out on my own, it would have taken much longer—plus I wouldn't have had the power of this new network.

Q: What kept you engaged in the group?

Varelie: I loved having a sounding board and access to some of the most creative people I've ever met. Being part of a group that was always coming up with innovative solutions to their own or other people's challenges was invigorating. I guess, to answer your question, I was pushed outside my comfort zone and learning new things.

Replace the Three Rs (References, Referrals, Recommendations) with the Two Cs: Collaboration and Crowdsourcing

House of Genius's Jonathan Beninson believes two things create community: working collaboratively to solve a problem and suffering together toward a common goal. In his mind, anything else is a fleeting alliance or filling a transactional need.

Simply asking for a reference or seeking a referral is an approach to networking that for some (Jonathan likely among them) feels stale—not necessarily old but definitely not what's truly effective today.

Look around you for a moment. A digital generation has grown up with the social tools and values inherent in a sharing culture, a generation that doesn't know what a job search was like before the open accessibility and searchability of LinkedIn.

For them, information is readily accessible in the cloud or accessed first from a community. They have grown up with a one-to-many model as the basis of social network relationship building, versus writing to a single pen pal. To riff on something my friend Andrew Grill, a global managing partner with IBM Social Consulting, likes to say, *It's a generation with an expectation about sharing, from sharing what they know, demanding sharing tools, and that others share too.*

It is this expectation of social collaboration in every aspect of their lives that fuels demand for more input, more social and collaboration tools, and more decentralized power within the group dynamic (whether it is at work or on their personal time). And as a result of the behaviors of this generation, the new networking is social, collaborative, and crowdsourced.

Where the Magic Really Happens

It is hard to imagine, but in 1999, when Tina Roth Eisenberg (aka @swissmiss) moved to New York City, she didn't know a soul.

Tina is a Swiss graphic designer with a growing number of varied business interests. There is *swissmiss*, her wildly popular design blog. There is TeuxDeux, a simple to-do app, and Tattly, temporary tattoos designed by a variety of talented designers. Then there is CreativeMornings, a network she launched to bring creative types together, which now spans the globe.

There are also her coworking spaces. Tina has cofounded two coworking spaces: Studiomates in 2008, which was replaced by Friends in 2015. The appearance of coworking spaces in every city neighborhood is a relatively new phenomenon. But Tina's desire to create her own workspace back in 2008 was not based on her, or anybody else's, need to find a desk to go to every day—once she started freelancing she easily found a "desk" (first at a drab software development firm on the Lower East Side, then with an architecture firm located in DUMBO); rather, it was based on her desire for the kind of collaboration that is only possible within a community.

Because what Tina had come to quickly realize (especially after working alongside epic individuals in a rules-centric workspace) was that the magic of being in a community doesn't come from having a desk in a cool space; it happens around the kitchen table.

For Tina, one lunch conversation turned into her task- and time-productivity app TeuxDeux. She was chatting about the pros and cons of various task-management apps, when a developer at the table chimed in, "Just design one and I will build it for you."

And she did.

But the point of creating "lunchtime conversations" is not to find someone who will build your app—it is the support that comes from being part of a community. Absurdly, Tina had never considered designing and building her own app. It took her community to show her that she could. And this story repeats itself for all of Tina's businesses to date, and she knows it will generate her future companies too.

When selecting a community to be part of, Tina advises:

- Surround yourself with people who give one another equal value and are inspired to do something together.
- Be thoughtful in building up your community. Fill it with people who allow one another to see bigger versions of themselves.
- Create water-cooler or "kitchen table" moments for your community, spaces and moments where interesting, engaging conversations can happen.

Determine Reputation and Visibility

Have you ever asked yourself, What, really, is the goal of X connections or Y followers or Z club memberships? Depending on how you analyze it, they are a sign either that you're completely distracted or that you're putting yourself in front of opportunity.

And what you need to be doing is visibly taking control of your opportunities by sharing (and shining a light on) what you know, because in a hyperconnected world chance encounters that make the right connection to the next opportunity don't happen by themselves. It's all about proactive visibility.

Varelie Croes admits that her promotion to director at PwC was fast-tracked because of her heightened visibility within the firm. During her eleven-year tenure, she organized events and ran different initiatives, enabling her to connect with leadership across the firm. PwC's Alternative Investments Seminar in particular put her on the senior leadership's radar and led to speaking opportunities in the private equity community as well as to her leading workshops for some of the biggest private equity funds in New York. Varelie didn't wait to be asked—she inserted herself into a community and put her knowledge in the spotlight.

Expert Insights: Invest the Time to Get on Board

In 2006, during her second year at the London College of Fashion, entrepreneur Devon Brooks carved out a completely innovative market category when she came up with the idea for Blo Blow Dry Bar (a no cuts or colors, blow-dry-only hair-styling salon). She opened the first location in Vancouver in early 2007. Blo now has fifty franchise locations across four countries and has also created opportunities for thousands of small-business owners and "competitor" brands operating in this new market category. Blo merged with another company in 2010, and Devon stepped back from day-to-day operations, but she didn't disappear from the business landscape.

Devon took her startup founder's experience—along with her ability to innovate industry standards, build scalable operating systems, and create a world-class corporate culture—and started mentoring other startup founders. She also started to plan and set her next professional goal in motion: a board seat on a prominent, national organization.

Proving you have the experience desired by a corporate board is just one of a long list of challenges to landing a coveted board seat. But perhaps the biggest challenge is successfully networking to make the board member connections, so you're top-of-mind if and when there is an open position. Relevant experience and desire is not enough to land a seat at the board table. You also have to ingratiate yourself into a notoriously closed-door club. (As one prominent female board member once said, "If you want to get on a corporate board, network with sixty-five-plus-year-old men.")

With determination and incredible focus, Devon has forged the right connections, in the right way, and achieved this, her next career goal.

Q: You're a member of the board of Futurpreneur Canada. Describe the organization. Why did you pursue a seat at that board table?

Devon: My filter on opportunities comes down to my legacy. I'm motivated by community and transformation. Futurpreneur Canada is an incredibly dynamic nonprofit organization that provides financing, mentoring, and business resources (like prelaunch coaching, business-plan-writing advice, workshops, and online tools) for aspiring entrepreneurs aged eighteen to thirty-nine. Canada is the second most entrepreneurially active G7 country in the world next to the United States, and younger generations are more entrepreneurially inclined; however, statistics show that 90 percent of startups fail. What can we do about that? I know from experience that entrepreneurs need superior support and education in order to see their businesses survive and thrive. Futurpreneur is focused on helping entrepreneurs succeed. It is a high-value, high-impact, high-integrity organization. Futurpreneur businesses have created more than thirty-one thousand jobs; its business-plan writer has been used by more than fifty thousand aspiring entrepreneurs; and 40 percent of the participating entrepreneurs are women. Through my work there, initially as a mentor and now as a board member, I am able to impact what my country, and the world, needs more of.

Q: Initially, your involvement with Futurpreneur Canada was as a business and leadership mentor. What made you want to take your engagement the step further to becoming a board member?

Devon: In terms of my own development, I wanted a new challenge and on a different scale. I had joined Futurpreneur as a mentor when I was twenty-three. After about two years of mentoring, I was sure I wanted to be on the board, and started deepening my involvement so I could better understand the organization as well as its needs. At that point my advocacy work had earned me an invitation to my first board experience at a Vancouver-based rape crisis center. After two years of a very active seat on that board, I was confident I had garnered enough knowledge to move to another, bigger organization. Simultaneously Futurpreneur was going through a massive shift: new management and a new CEO. Of course the board led much of the search for these new roles. In 2013, under the direction of the new CEO, the organization had evolved and rebranded. And it was at that point I was certain my skills and experience would be valued by the board (not to mention adding diversity to the board's composition)—so I began to actively pursue a Futurpreneur board position, successfully joining the board in 2015.

Q: Becoming a board member didn't happen overnight or simply because you raised your hand. Once you identified your goal of attaining a board seat, what was your approach and strategy to being nominated for the board?

Devon: You've heard the saying "It takes twenty years to become an overnight success"? Well, for me it didn't take nearly that long to earn a spot where I wanted one, but I like how that saying speaks to persistence and patience. It requires concerted action and clear intention to achieve, and experience, whatever it is that you desire. For me, the journey from idea to invitation to become a board member was four years (not including the two years I had previously spent as a mentor for the organization).

When I became an entrepreneur I saw firsthand the important role boards play in companies staying aligned to their vision and strategy. Being on a board of directors is a very unique environment—it is a collective of talented individuals from a broad range of disciplines, with a wide variety of perspectives, coming together to provide a very high-level kind of guidance. It requires emotional intelligence, tact, a deep understanding of the organization at hand, and an equally deep understanding of your role and liability as a board member.

I made time to get to know Futurpreneur's local team members and leadership team, plus to build a strong rapport with the CEO and several board members. I was attentive to Futurpreneur, offering my time and skill when the organization was going through significant changes. I worked with the team at large, as a mentor, whenever I could so that I fully appreciated the impact of the organization. It was an intentional and comprehensive approach. When the board was ready to look at new members, I wholeheartedly wanted to be at the top of their list.

Q: Understanding you had no control over the length of the board nomination process or timing for appointments, how did you manage to stay top-of-mind with the board members you met with?

Devon: Service and relationships. Continuing to proactively serve and offer support to members of the organization. Everything from leaning into a marketing brainstorm with some seasoned advice to making introductions to forward the team's agenda. Maintaining and nurturing relationships takes thoughtfulness. It doesn't mean nonsensical, or overly casual, check-ins and e-mail updates; it means learning to ask the right questions so you can discern how your time can be best used to forward that relationship. It means always communicating with intention to add value.

Q: You're active online and a frequent keynote speaker. How did these activities fit into your journey to the boardroom? How else did you socialize your desire to be considered a board member?

Devon: Because I am clear on my greater purpose I filter everything through the same lens of transformation and community.

I say yes to the gigs supporting that and no to the ones that don't.

The socializing component was a no-brainer and I think it should feel like a no-brainer if you are going after the right things. When you are connecting with someone, or a roomful of people, over something you care about (and are genuinely knowledgeable and curious about), you will continually find yourself in the right rooms, with the right people. And when you build relationships over a shared purpose it elevates everyone involved.

Q: Any other networking guidance for others who have similar goals or ambitions?

Devon: If you think you are the smartest person in the room, you are truly an idiot.

Q: Generosity is an important networking concept. How did it play out in your Futurpreneur networking activities?

Devon: Generosity of spirit is often defined as giving more than is necessary or expected, or living from the inside out. When I invest in relationships or new opportunities, I am very decisive about what's important, and I will do whatever serves the higher purpose. I feel like the value I receive is the result of the integrity of what I put in. At least I hope that's what someone might say about me.

Put Yourself in Front of Opportunity

If you've got a defined goal like Devon did, you need to set out to make it happen. While we all like to be recognized for our actions and chosen for leadership positions, waiting to be acknowledged or selected has no place when it comes to reaching for your goals. Once you know what you're capable of and want to achieve, it's essential to proactively take control by sharing that information across the right networking channels and into targeted communities.

The networking instinct to share (more than selfies) is essential for a job-jumping generation. A status update is networking, as is tagging your expertise on an internal social network. Internal social networks also tell a bigger story, beyond your skills, know-how, and expertise—they indicate who's a team player, which matters too, especially now as employers seek out the connectors within their organizations and jobs requiring social skills are rewarded more than those involving routine functions.

Networking events such as a panel discussion or keynote conversation where the moderator "opens the floor to questions" are opportunities to share your knowledge or shine a light on your interests. During Q&A sessions, use the microphone to your advantage, as all the attendees, from the influencers to your peers, are looking at you. Remember to tell people who you are by stating your name. Tell people what you do (role, company, department), then ask your question in a clear and precise manner. Remember to be quotable! It's a 140-character world—rambling and run-on sentences are a thing of the past and don't have great networking impact.

The Next Big Thing: What Makes Ideas Happen?

Ideas don't come to life on their own. They need community. Without community, Tina's simple, designy to-do app wouldn't exist. Kathryn wouldn't have successfully crowdfunded a documentary. Joe wouldn't have mastered the skills he needed to land a coveted managerial job.

Ideas also require us to trust in the extended power of the community.

Remember, there is massive potential behind each and every person in a community or organization—and networking serendipity powerfully comes into play when the right contact or lead results from an unlikely or overlooked source. Adopt the House of Genius mentality: everyone has genius inside them and all ideas are equal.

If you want to make your next big thing happen, move beyond surface assumptions and knee-jerk conclusions.

Business Bonds, Not BFFs

Participating in an angel-investment group was another career aha! moment for me. I realized a lot about what I had the potential to do—early-stage investing—all because of the learning and interaction that occurred among like-minded individuals in a group setting. When others have asked me about the experience, they often assume other social needs were fulfilled by my decision to join, or at least contributed to my enthusiasm for the experience. But for me a group-learning environment and set "class" schedule was the motivation I needed to learn about angel investing. I wasn't looking to form lasting friendships—I only wanted to connect with a group of women investors whose investment judgment I respected so we could productively work together toward a unanimous investment decision. Nothing more to it than that. And once the boot camp was over and the investment decision was made, I had very little reason to continue to engage with the group.

Don't confuse a group's purpose and try to expand it into something it isn't.

That said, there are definitely times when you can convince a group of people to try a different approach to solving a problem. Chattanooga's JumpFund is just one such example: it took a philanthropic group of women and turned them into angel investors.

The JumpFund started over a lunch conversation at Whole Foods. From that lunch, the idea that there should be a fund focused on investing in women gained traction with other women in the community, ultimately leading to a $2.4 million Chattanooga-based early-stage investment fund. The general partners of the fund were able to successfully coalesce a traditionally community-focused group of new investors around a new mission: creating jobs and serving the community by investing in women-owned businesses (versus focusing solely on charitable efforts to improve the lives of women in the community). All the JumpFund investors are women with one thing in common: a desire to elevate women in business.

Initially, the fund's general partners did not know if Chattanooga was ready for the JumpFund, and they spent almost a year meeting with women in the community—women who had primarily been prominent in business or community service or charitable activities. Seeing early-stage investment as a path to achieving a shared goal (beyond the diverse approaches of charitable or government-supported initiatives they had been taking previously) was the key to success, and the general partners were ultimately able to recruit forty-five women as limited partners for the first fund.

Values and Volunteers

The spark for CreativeMornings (a monthly breakfast networking event for creative types, now operating in 130 cities around the globe) were the comments left on Tina Roth Eisenberg's popular design blog, *swissmiss*, after she posted about a conference she'd recently attended. Comments like "You're so lucky," "My boss wouldn't let me attend," and "I couldn't afford the ticket price" made Tina feel badly about the disparity in the creative community: those who could benefit the most from the events she was attending were those least likely to be able to go. Her solution was to create a free monthly event that anyone in the creative community could attend.

Tina admits that the first event was a bit awkward: there was no focus, just networking. Now every CreativeMornings event has a speaker, and every month the presentations have a different theme. Time, humility, revolution, empathy, and work are just a few of the past themes. All this helps Tina to realize her simple mission of getting people together to talk, and to see what happens from there. Nothing more, and nothing less valuable, than that.

So what explains the phenomenal growth of Creative-Mornings, if it's not the speakers or themes or sponsors or free breakfast? Values. CreativeMornings is a community built entirely on generosity and trust, not tit-for-tat transactional expectations, which likely explains why many first-time attendees are mildly suspicious, wondering where's the catch at the end of the free breakfast.

While there are eight salaried employees at CreativeMornings, the strength of the community truly rests on the generosity of 145 city hosts and more than 1,400 event assistants, all of whom volunteer their time willingly each month. Every decision Tina and her team at CreativeMornings makes is first analyzed through the lens of how it will impact these volunteers. As Tina bluntly states it, "We cannot piss off the bottom layer." It's this accountability to the community volunteers and the trust those volunteers have in Tina and her team that keep CreativeMornings growing.

The Dream Crowd

Often we are dazzled by the description of a community, while neglecting to see whether it is capable of fulfilling its promise.

I was invited to an exclusive networking opportunity with billionaires, corporate executives, and leading health-care-technology innovators. The multiday event held out much promise for dynamic conversation, given the access and isolated location. The problem? No one was really quite sure who was actually attending the event. Introductions were left to chance, as the organizers were overly reliant on connecting people via an app—and exclusively via that app. I can only conclude that the app made the conference administrators' lives easier, because it did not improve the experience for the attendees.

The app was essentially void of basic contact information (seems obvious but let me say it: an elite group of individuals is highly unlikely to make their image and personal contact information visible on an app downloadable to any smartphone), leading to a lot of questioning of the true value of the event and whether the promised influential subset of the community was truly in attendance.

Overreliance on technology often leads to overlooking the very human nature of connecting, and in this scenario it completely overlooked the social dynamics and needs of this particular group of people. Members of this self-selected group were seeking a high-touch and hands-on approach to networking. They wanted the high-touch confirmation that only comes with personalized face-to-face introductions made by a trusted source. They were not looking for yet another networking app.

The result? A rapid downhill spiral of trust in the event's promise—as well as a constant questioning of the power of the community behind it. I'm not sure if the event organizers were distrustful of those who showed up or simply top-down control freaks about their most valuable contacts—whatever the explanation, this, unfortunately, is the networking atmosphere they unwittingly created (and it will be a hard one to correct).

To bring a self-selecting group together once is a singular achievement; to provide an experience that is valuable and useful to that group is much more difficult to consistently accomplish! So difficult, most people get it wrong—they seek ease and shortcuts when, you guessed it, there is nothing easy about building connections.

To engage a community so deeply that it wants to keep coming back, you need to stay singularly focused on its networking needs. Get it right from the start, because community dynamics (like corporate culture) are hard to change over time.

What, then, is really a dream crowd? It has nothing to do with billionaires or celebrity or access to exclusive venues, and it has everything to do with:

- A community that consistently delivers on its original promise to its members

- A community of a size and composition that enables you to achieve your goal (for Varelie, it was a mastermind group; for Tina, a coworking space of thirty people)
- A community that embraces the value of generosity to enable the beneficial features of the group to scale

Grassroots Growth Takes Effort

Before you sign on, understand the effort needed for the community to be successful. And I'm referring equally to the efforts of the organizers and the participants. Because being part of, or creating, community is never effortless—it is individual effort within a team interaction.

The reason 85 Broads worked was because its membership was motivated and driven. CreativeMornings is relentless in maintaining the trust of its 1,400 volunteers and 145 local leaders because the success of the community depends on it being an engine of generosity. Evan Nisselson rises above the networking noise by constantly providing value, from monthly dinner gathering to monthly dinner gathering (and by only inviting individuals who understand the need for an ongoing generous and mutual exchange of value).

House of Genius is built upon the premise that people want to connect—with a structured, rules-based twist. Connections made within the House of Genius community start on a foundation of anonymity and an understanding that all ideas are equal in value. House of Genius has rules of engagement: drop your status and leave your business cards and ego at the door. The conversation is always moderated, and agreement is declared by stating "plus one" rather than using it as an opportunity for extended commentary or mic dropping. The rules keep the commentary fresh and the playing field equal. Make no mistake, however: creating an environment where everyone understands that every person at the table has genius to share requires mutual effort. And the House of Genius rules aren't for everyone.

Before you join a community, consider whether you're up to making the effort.

Start, Incubate, Accelerate

IBM's Millennial Corps started as a result of its partnership with Apple—and the need to create one hundred enterprise apps. As millennials use apps intuitively and are the first generation to understand that smartphones can be figured out without a physical instruction manual (or the need to refer to a Q&A section on a website), IBM decided to turn to the millennials in its workforce for feedback in the creation of these apps.

The thousand participants in the app project liked being part of a community within the larger organization—so much so that they self-organized and continued the online group as a place to convene and share ideas related to the business or workplace. IBM's Millennial Corps is now an internal network of four thousand members in sixty-one countries.

And its success has also lead to #500under40,[21] a series of networking events for IBM's Millennial Corps with their peers from other Fortune 500 companies (the first event in New York City included millennial employees from nine different Fortune 500 companies, including Ernst & Young, Estée Lauder, PepsiCo, and MetLife). The organizers recognized that in a few years millennials would be the decision makers within the businesses (as well as training the next generation in the workforce). As such, fostering collaboration and building peer networks is essential for their professional growth as leaders, as well as for the longer-term success of the business.

The networks and connections you need to accelerate your future have to be built now (I know I'm a broken record on this point). However, before agonizing over who should be in the network or what it should focus on, try bringing a few colleagues or a loosely knit collection of like-minded individuals together around a business need or community project before you lay down the rules of engagement or plan the first event.

Technology may be driving rapid change, but what innovation in business needs now is collaboration, communication, and creativity—aka people! And some of the most important connections you'll ever make will be in the workplace.

Still not convinced you need to pay close attention to interactions in the workplace?

- If you're actively searching for a job, then you should be focusing on your social skills and your ability to work with others! Nearly all job growth since 1980 has been in social-skill-intensive occupations. This economy-wide shift is rewarding those with strong social skills up and down the corporate ladder.[22]
- Social connections might just be the new double bottom line. According to Gallup, having close friends and positive interactions at work significantly increases engagement with the organization, as strong relationships at work anchor people's commitment to the organization, its brand,

and its purpose. Yes! There is finally empirical data that being social at work is actually good for employees and organizations![23]

■ The growing importance of social skills in the workplace is directly related to disruptive technology that has shifted the organization of work toward flexible and self-managed team structures, job rotation, and worker multitasking.[24]

Expert Insights: Success Isn't Just about the Idea—It's about Investing Time in the Network

In ten years, the venture capital firm First Round Capital has built an enviable reputation in the startup community, not only because of its portfolio of more than three hundred innovative, emerging tech companies (it was one of the first investors in Uber), but also on the strength of its network. First Round has invested significant amounts of time and consideration in its community. And that investment is paying off. The engagement it has facilitated between the founders of its portfolio companies enables the six-partner firm to scale in ways others can only dream of. Every early-stage investor wants to see its founders succeed; however, while it is not humanly possible for six partners to be there 24-7 for each and every one of those founders, the firm can, by having a community genuinely invested in one another's success, literally always be there for each and every portfolio company. With the scale of community, First Round provides necessary guidance at each critical stage in a startup's journey. Fostering an ethos of generosity in their network leaves the partners of the firm able to make high-impact ad hoc connections too. And the lasting bonds the members of its community have created—as mentors, as advisors, and as friends—thrills First Round, as this is the "frothy" dynamic of networks that has led to Silicon Valley's unparalleled economic success.

To understand what makes First Round—as a venture firm and as a community of venture-backed companies—tick, I sought out the partner located at the center of interconnected innovation networks: San Francisco–based Rob Hayes. Rob joined First Round in 2006, opening the firm's San Francisco office. Rob led First Round's investment in Uber (as well as Mint and Square, among others). A longtime investor, Rob has a keen interest in sharing-economy companies and a strong belief that great ideas can come from anywhere.

Q: First Round Capital has an enviable peer-to-peer community of startup CEOs and CMOs, and building this community within its portfolio companies has been a foundation of First Round's operational structure since the firm launched. Why is that?

Rob: When you look at the traditional venture capital model, you see the partners at the center of everything. All the companies are connected through the partner, so whenever they're looking for advice or to tap into resources, they have to go to that partner to access the information or introduction they need. This isn't scalable, and given the fact that we're a seed-stage firm with over three hundred investments, we needed a more efficient system where we could serve all our companies better with the same number of partners.

Our solution has been to build the tools, events, and software for members of First Round companies (not just CEOs and founders) to connect directly with their peers at other companies in our community. These are the folks who are operating on the ground today and have the latest knowledge and expertise that they can share directly with their peers. This has scaled our ability to deliver high-quality, relevant, targeted help significantly. Given that our mission is to build and serve the strongest possible community of entrepreneurs, having this leverage has been vital.

Q: Can you describe how hands-on you and other First Round partners are with the portfolio companies and how your role evolves over time (or funding rounds)?

Rob: We're incredibly entrepreneur-centric and committed to doing everything we can to help companies succeed, especially within their first eighteen months. That's where we excel—helping founders at that point when every decision they make dramatically impacts the trajectory of their companies. First Round partners often sit on boards during this time period to provide guidance and support. Our doors are always open to meet with entrepreneurs and help them troubleshoot specific problems—perhaps the most special thing about it is that this support is unwavering as our companies grow. We've even hosted a number of companies at our three offices before they had spaces of their own.

Q: Ten years of community building is a lifetime in the evolution of networking online. Any reflections on how social media and community platforms have influenced your approach to community engagement?

Rob: As with everything we do here at First Round, we try to provide unique value. So while we've steered away from pulling the typical levers, we have thought about trends and how we can take them the distance to benefit our startups and entre-preneurs. Two efforts come to mind: *First Round Review* and First Round Network.

When we launched *First Round Review*[25] in the summer of 2013, the content-marketing trend was only just starting and wasn't nearly the constant presence it is today. We simply saw how important it would be to get in front of as many brilliant founders and prospective entrepreneurs as possible. So we hit on this recipe to publish long-form interviews with tech leaders sharing tactical lessons from their experience with the general public. It has completely transformed engagement on our social channels (especially Twitter and LinkedIn) and has added a whole new dimension to the First Round brand.

First Round Network is our home-built social network (with functionality similar to Quora). Not only does it allow people to ask and answer questions, it also hosts a series of step-by-step guides for our companies to think through thorny issues. We also use it to host live Q&A sessions. I think we were also pretty prescient here, as more platforms like Product Hunt, Growth-Hackers, and others have sprung up since, to foster dialogue between startups.

Q: How else do you facilitate peer connections for your in-vestments?

Rob: A couple of our programs come to mind here. The First Round Expert Network is a relatively new database of now over 250 remarkable professionals who have had numerous successes across functional areas—HR, design, product, engineering, man-agement, etc. And all of them are excited and eager to share their knowledge with less-experienced founders and employees at startups in our community. It's filling a need that I don't think anyone knew was there. Traditional startup advising is largely broken, and people rarely get the full value of their advisors. By tapping into the Expert Network engagements, First Round portfolio companies can work through specific problems on a set timetable with someone superqualified to help them solve it.

The second is our extensive Knowledge Program, which focuses on facilitating offline connections. Last year alone, First Round hosted more than eighty events—literally an event every couple of days—where we invited people to meaningfully connect and share knowledge with their peers. Most of these events take the form of salons—small, guided dinner discussions of fourteen to twenty people who all work in the same area. We convene a mix of the most brilliant people we know across the entire ecosystem with members of First Round companies.

Q: How does First Round manage the peer network? What apps, platforms, or other mechanisms (online and offline) do you rely on? How do you decide which to use or try? What data points do you pay attention to?

Rob: Our network is extremely dependent on high-quality personal relationships. I've mentioned First Round Network, our software that connects people at our many companies together for the purposes of getting advice. We have vibrant and large social media channels—we currently have more than 130,000 followers on Twitter. And we have our robust event program that brings different groups of people together regularly in person.

We're also constantly looking at how often different members of our community are contacted. We want to make sure that we're always giving more to people than we're asking of them. We use tools like Datahug to record our touchpoints with people and make sure that our relationship is strong, recent, and positive. This allows us to make better peer-to-peer introductions when the time is right.

Q: As a great friend of mine once said, "The network is incomplete or useless until you bring it offline." How is First Round connecting its portfolio companies offline?

Rob: Our most significant offline engagement is our Knowledge Program, which brings people together for dozens of guided conversations over dinner, at major summits attended by hundreds of tech leaders, and through other occasions in between. The key differentiator for us is that we don't simply invite people to network over cocktails. We don't leave a group to its own devices, and we don't run events for purely social purposes. We want everything we do to add value for the people who attend, which means really understanding what they need and how best to deliver it to them.

Q: What's surprised you about the community?

Rob: I continue to be surprised by how willing members of our community are to give their time and offer their wisdom. These are extremely busy, driven people who are constantly working at max capacity. So to see how generously they'll take time out of their day to help another entrepreneur overcome a challenge or solve a problem is completely awesome. I think it speaks to how easy we make it for people to find each other and share what they know. Our programs are all designed to make knowledge share a low-lift, extremely positive experience.

Q: What guidance do you have for others about when to actively manage a community and when to get out of the way? How can you tell if you're providing value to the community?

Rob: Your job is really to provide a framework that enables high-value interactions. This is how we think about our events and First Round Network. We want to create a structure, tools, and ground rules that let people engage in meaningful dialogue with people who are proven experts. That's one of the things that makes our peer network so strong—we're very focused on connecting them with the exact right domain expert who can speak from experience. So I'd argue that you want to play a role as a curator focused on the dynamics of relationships. And the best way to figure out if you are adding value is through both systematic surveys and the rigorous collection of voluntary feedback.

Q: Others in venture capital have tried to establish peer-to-peer networks with limited success. Any thoughts on why top-down community efforts flop?

Rob: It takes a commitment of resources and time. We've really invested in creating this peer network in a big way. This means running experiments, taking risks, and not expecting things to pay off immediately. When *First Round Review* started, it was a huge experiment. We wrote some articles and waited to see engagement. When we did, we put a bunch of resources behind it to make it the site it is today. Likewise, with First Round Network, we started with a very casual Yahoo group that connected the founders of our companies. It was so embraced that we built on it more and more. In both these cases and others, we tested, tried new things again and again, pivoted, collected feedback, and tried again. If other peer networks are failing, I would wager it's because this type of investment hasn't been made. It's the only way that we've found such precise product-market fit with so many of our programs.

Networks You Need

If I were to keep my most important contacts on a spreadsheet, I'd find myself spending more time creating spreadsheets than actually getting things done.

Don't get me wrong! I do believe that some of us are fortunate enough in our professional lives to find that lifelong mentor or small group of long-term advisors. Yet, for more of us, as our careers evolve and increasingly include a variety of personal projects and a lot of side hustle, we will be constantly gathering allies and joining groups in order to make additional contacts around the needs we have at different points in time in our professional lives.

The key is finding and effectively accessing the networks you need at the times you need their advice, guidance, and support most. And it's not just about the guidance or support you're seeking—it is also about maximizing your time. As you've likely realized at this point, there is no magic time-saving bullet for building strong connections, other than being smarter by taking control of the networking process and your intended outcomes.

Here's a do-some-diligence checklist before joining a group or signing up on the membership dotted line:

* Ask yourself why. What is it you are trying to achieve (your "goal") and why is this the group or community to help you achieve it?

- What's the focus for the group (social or business, long-term business growth or short-term project) and how does that align with your goal?
- Check the "rules of engagement." Can you reach your goal within their system or structure?
- What's the group's track record? Does it align with the current promise of membership and lay a strong foundation for ongoing delivery of its commitment to members?
- Do the individual members of the group share the networking culture of the group?
- Do you have the slightest interest in or passion for the group beyond seeing it as a vehicle to achieve your goal?
- Is there a platform (online or off) where the group can convene and share ideas?

5

#Networking

SOCIAL VERSUS IRL: using one without the other doesn't harness the whole.

Technology has opened our lives to more opportunities to connect—to people, ideas, distractions, time wasters, and innovation. It has expanded the tools and networking venues. It has changed how we stay in touch with people in our lives. We used to have to wait ten, twenty-five, or thirty years to awkwardly gather in a school gym to discover what happened to our classmates from high school or college. Oh, how with technology have the times changed for the better! The bonds we create through shared struggles and accomplishments are some of the strongest we'll ever make.

The challenge is in finding ways for technology to work with you, not at you.

Just for a moment, however, let's forget social networking platforms or contact-sorting productivity apps, to focus on this:

- When are you most productive?
- Where do your best ideas come from?
- Who do you seek out for insights?

Now consider the people you immediately turn to for advice or to share a joke. Have you ever taken the time to really pay attention to how your closest friends or your wider community of contacts connect, communicate, and engage on social platforms? How, when, and where we put out content is strong signaling on how, when, and where to connect.

One seventy-year-old grandmother I know definitely breaks stereotypes: based in Silicon Valley, she's an early tech adopter *and* an avid NFL fan. At a Sunday brunch I can guarantee her eyes will be glued to multiple screens for updates on all the games (not just her beloved 49ers), and the conversation will focus on how she is doing in her fantasy football league. This won't be the time to approach her for stories from her youth.

Observe, don't assume. Use the valuable data people are giving you to connect with them more effectively. Drop your assumptions about how and where you think people network, and instead pay close attention to how they are really connecting. How your connections embrace technology (posts, tweets, texts, e-mails, updates, mobile, tablet) indicates what matters to them and how, when, and where they want to connect. The same goes for the people you want to network with.

Technology use reveals the mundane, delightful, and unexpected. It's simply a matter of pausing to take a greater interest in the behaviors and habits of people on those platforms, instead of focusing on the functionality of the platform itself.

The Not-So-Early Adopter

I've come to realize that to produce my best work I need to be selective about what invades my inbox and monopolizes my computer screen (or the home screen on my mobile phone). If I'm not the "first to know," so be it, and FOMO be darned. I've also realized that I'm not an early adopter. I was still using a BlackBerry until 2012. I have downloaded a select few apps to my iPhone and use even a smaller number of those apps daily. While I tweet, blog, and send out a weekly e-mail newsletter, I will never find my name on a "pioneer in the digital field" list. I don't have a YouTube channel or my own podcast (yet). Finally, I don't aspire to be a source for breaking news (we have CNN and Fox News or, more than likely, Twitter for that).

I realize I'm sounding perfectly Neanderthal, especially for someone who has fully embraced online platforms as useful networking venues. I recognize the massive value of connecting with social media; however, I have to use it in a way that is valuable to me—in a way that fits with my work style and lifestyle.

Social media is not going away (as the "I don't get it" crowd may wish). It is now possible to text, post, and tweet from Mount Everest, so there is truly no escaping it! Not being on social media excludes *you*—your goals, ambitions, talents—from opportunities to connect. It is letting your opportunities be defined without your participation in creating them for yourself.

Social media is powerful. Used intentionally, it enables meaningful human connections, rather than detracting from them. It creates more opportunities for conversations and enables new ideas to take hold (which may explain why some people don't get it).

Coffee Talk

Twitter was not the first social networking "threat" to the established rules of how to start a conversation. And Snapchat,

Confide, Yammer, Yik Yak, HipChat, Viber, and WhatsApp won't be the last.

Social networking, in the form of coffeehouses, threatened the fabric of productive society starting in the 1600s. Coffeehouses were popular places to go to read pamphlets and learn the news. They were the de facto post offices and open places to communicate and exchange new ideas. Coffeehouses, like social networking platforms today, democratized networking. By 1739, coffeehouses in London numbered around 550 (before giving way to the tea trend and the rise of private clubs for men).[26]

With the surge in entrepreneurial activity, we have returned to "coffeehouses" and the desire to work alongside other similarly minded individuals productively. Ideas need contact and community to become something more than just an idea. Coffeehouses, by providing an open space for ideas to be exchanged, facilitated the creation of new communities and, more important, for new ideas to take hold.

Discussion, debate, discourse—these human interactions transform thinking about an idea into pursuing that idea. Today our coffeehouses are Twitter, LinkedIn, Facebook, Tumblr, Instagram, Pinterest, WordPress, GitHub, Asana, Trello, Slack . . . plus hackathons, coworking spaces and coworking communities (such as Friends), meetups, incubator and accelerator programs, and hotel lobbies with free Wi-Fi (walk into the Ace Hotel in New York City on any given day to see what I mean). Even corporations are trying to become coffeehouses, as they shift to open floor plans and away from private offices and assigned workspaces.

Such "coffeehouses" are a cornerstone of innovation and creativity, not simply because the physical environment permits the exchange of ideas, but because of who chooses to be in the "coffee

shop," exchanging ideas. In the seventeenth century, social dis-
tinctions were not recognized within the walls of coffeehouses—
they were open to anyone (well, except women). They were truly
public places (for the times), where anyone could gather and
share ideas. This is why coffeehouses were perceived to be dan-
gerous, a threat to society.

A venue that permits anyone to come in and share ideas
sounds a bit like Twitter, doesn't it?

Twitter created the popular coffeehouse genre for the digital
age—a platform where we could speak directly with anyone. In
my own experience, I've "chatted" with Tom Peters, listened in to
exchanges with fierce investigative minds like finance/business
editor Heidi Moore, ventured between entrepreneurial communities with author and Foreign Policy Interrupted cofounder Elmira
Bayrasli, challenged entrenched notions on corporate governance
alongside board member Lucy Marcus, and watched newswor-
thy and other worldly events unfold. My Saturday morning frequently starts with a "coffee chat" alongside friends @lucymarcus,
@endeavoringE, and @amyresnick. Quite simply, I've diversified
my insights, found opportunities, and shared more than a few
laughs by observing and being part of the conversations going on
in this open and global "coffeehouse."

For most of us, it is not a question of whether we're hanging
out in "coffeehouses" anymore; rather it's a question of whether
we are communicating and sharing information in such a way
that others want to listen to what we have to say. Equally, we
need to fight that natural human instinct to continually seek the
comfort of the familiar seat and rehash the news with the same
group of people.

On that note, who did you sit next to in the library or chat
with on Slack or hashtag on a corporate intranet yesterday?

Look around the "coffeehouses" you're frequenting IRL or online. If you're seeing the same faces day after day and are looking forward to having the conversation you had the day before, then you're not networking where you need to be. Picking up where you left off may be keeping you behind.

To Connect or Not to Connect

Confession: I ignore LinkedIn connection requests.

I'm a fan of LinkedIn. The platform is a valuable way to expand a professional network; however, networking needs, like careers, evolve, pivot, shift, and transition. My own approach to connecting on LinkedIn has evolved, just as my participation in networking groups and membership in industry associations have. Networking is not a static activity!

I started actively and aggressively using LinkedIn when I was manager of alumni programs at White & Case. Tasked with rebuilding the global alumni network, I needed to find and connect with the firm's alums. What better place to do that than on LinkedIn, as well as Facebook and, to a lesser degree, other closed or industry-focused social networking platforms? I connected with a lot of people in order to get my job done. I shared a loose trust bond with hundreds if not thousands of connections based on having the same employer listed on our online profile—but I cannot honestly say I know these people.

That was how I used LinkedIn in the years 2008 and 2009. When I moved on from that job and my networking focus shifted, there was no need to have all those loose connections based solely on the shared experience of a former employer. From

2009 to 2010, I was president of 85 Broads. From time to time during that year, I grabbed a consulting project with a law firm or delivered a networking presentation at a Fortune 500 company. Casting my networking connections net broadly became a new-business-pipeline necessity for me. I actively connected with anyone I met and shook hands with at a networking event. I needed a wider network to feed me information and opportunities as I moved forward professionally from the life of a paycheck to one relying on short-term projects.

Fast forward to today. It should be rather clear that my reputation and my career momentum rest squarely on my network. That's a responsibility I take seriously. Connecting now feels like handing over the keys to a vault where I store all my most valued possessions.

I started advising and investing in startups in 2012—solely as a result of my network. I'm being asked to speak at conferences and to deliver keynotes, again because of introductions that have come through my network. My network has always fueled my career and fed me opportunities. It was no less valuable in 2008, but something has definitely shifted. I'm now much more selective about whom I connect with and whom I put my word, my reputation, my tweet on the line for.

Can I vouch for you? Really? Do you care about my relationships and value my connections as much as I do? Maybe? Or maybe not. Are you looking for a quick-hit intro or a long-term professional connection? These are some of the questions that pop into my mind when I see an "I'd like to add you to my professional network on LinkedIn" message, with nothing more.

Think about your own social interactions.

You may have had a lively conversation with someone at

a networking event, but was your interaction anything more than that? Who knows? Perhaps you'll find out the next time you cross paths with that person. Is it a charade to connect, to say you're "friends" or "professional connections" with someone when you likely don't know more about that person than where you met and perhaps what beverage they were drinking out of a plastic cup? You may share an interest in mobile technology or designer shoes or ice hockey or art or corporate governance, but is that reason enough to connect on a social networking site?

I don't have the answer; I'm just suggesting you think about the question. The functionality of the platform may facilitate connections, but it doesn't necessarily ease the friction of *why* we connect.

Virtual Is Reality

Lots of people doubt the power of social media, but Elena Rossini is not one of them. The Paris-based Italian filmmaker truly loves Twitter—so much so, she has four accounts on the social networking platform.

Interestingly, Elena and I did not meet on Twitter (although it has definitely enhanced our long-distance friendship); instead, we met when she reached out to interview me for her blog *No Country for Young Women*. That was back in 2010, and while travels occasionally permit us to catch up over a glass of champagne, we rely heavily on social media to stay on top of each other's numerous projects.

Beyond being a communication channel with friends, Twitter has been a vital source of business for Elena. She not only reached a crowdfunding target with the assistance of the platform but subsequently secured screenings for her independent documentary *The Illusionists* using Twitter. Elena juggles freelance projects as a videographer, photographer, and writer when she's not pursuing her own projects. Twitter provides her more leads than any help-wanted ad, but it all comes down to what she has to offer and how she engages with others in this online room. Whether she is tweeting with friends, media, or global brands, her approach is consistently genuine, enthusiastic, and conversational (which likely accounts for her success).

Q: How many opportunities have come to you through networking on Twitter?

Elena: I estimate that more than 80 percent of the job opportunities I have had in the past four years have come to me through Twitter. Aside from my feature-length documentary, all the freelance filmmaking projects I had in 2015 are a direct result of companies noticing me on Twitter and asking me to work for them.

When it comes to press coverage, the number is close to 99 percent. As a direct result of reaching out to journalists on Twitter, I have had numerous features about my work in publications like *Vogue Italia*, *New York* magazine's *The Cut*, *Il Sole 24 Ore* (Italy's equivalent of the *Wall Street Journal*), and the blog *Jezebel*, just to mention a few.

Q: I think of Twitter as a cocktail party. Describe how you approach Twitter as a networking platform.

Elena: Many people dismiss Twitter as a time waster and something narcissistic, devoid of value. I think it depends on how you use it and the kind of people you follow. For me, Twitter has been an excellent tool to get my work noticed and to connect with many inspiring people who have eventually become friends in real life.

I have a specific way of reading and writing messages on Twitter. As a reader, the most useful tool I have found is lists: I sort people, companies, and organizations in topical lists (for instance "people in film," "body image activists," "journalists," "gender equality advocates," or simply "interesting"), so that when I check out a particular stream, it's generally on point and doesn't feel like endless, disorganized chatter.

When I tweet, I try to be consistent in the content of my messages. I've found that people on Twitter generally don't like dealing with too many subjects. The account for my documentary (@illusionists) has over 8,800 followers, and my series of interviews with women about their professional lives on *No Country for Young Women* (@NCYW) has more than 12,000 followers. Of course, @illusionists is all about body image and media literacy and @NCYW is about women's empowerment and social justice. My personal Twitter account, @_elena, by contrast, only has about 3,000 followers, even though I started it a full two years before the other two accounts! I think what makes the other two accounts grow—and they do, even when I've been away for a while—is the fact they are seen as "expert voices" on those subjects.

Q: How have you been so successful in connecting with CEOs and journalists, when so many people fail to really connect? Describe your approach and strategy.

Elena: I believe a positive, constructive attitude is the reason why I have been so successful on Twitter. I never use it to vent or engage in negative talk. I try to provide valuable information regarding topics like body image activism (@illusionists) or celebrate inspiring women around the world (@NCYW).

Q: How does online networking download into the real world for you? Is there a distinction anymore between networking online and networking offline?

Elena: Following up Twitter conversations with real-life meetings has always been essential to me to cement relationships. I have met many incredible people at conferences: I would sit in the audience and live-tweet interesting panel discussions, always making sure to include the Twitter handle of the panelists onstage. This has often led to messages thanking me and asking to have a chat over coffee during the conference. This is an example of how the two experiences (online and offline) can complement each other.

Q: Walk us through how you met the CEO of Lottie dolls and what a single tweet has led to.

Elena: In the summer of 2015, I was invited to speak at the Inspirefest conference in Dublin, Ireland. All the speakers received a goodie bag that included Lottie—a doll that looks like a real child and whose appeal is based on each doll's interests. One Lottie hunts for fossils, another rides horses, another does karate . . . the list goes on. I fell in love with Lottie at first sight. When I returned home after the conference and before unpacking my suitcase, I took a selfie in my home office with Lottie and tweeted this message:

> ❝
> *Totally smitten with my @Lottie_dolls* **a wonderful present to speakers at @InspirefestHQ** she now sits on my desk
> ❞

Lottie dolls' community managers not only retweeted my tweet almost immediately, they reached out to me, after researching my websites, blogs, and other Twitter accounts. I have to note that my mother, on the other hand, chided me for that tweet, saying: "Elena, you're an adult woman. What are you doing taking pictures with a doll and posting them online?"

Two months after my tweet, I received an e-mail from one of the cofounders of Lottie dolls, thanking me for my tweets and inviting me to collaborate with them. Creating a short documentary about Stargazer Lottie—the first doll in outer space— and the six-year-old girl who helped design it has been one of the most exciting job opportunities I've had.[27] Because of this project, which started on Twitter, I've had the opportunity to meet Claudie Haigneré, the first French female astronaut on the *International Space Station*. And, yes, my skeptical-about-social-media mom couldn't be more proud.

Q: Generosity is an important networking concept. How did it play out in your networking activities on Twitter?

Elena: I love to discover and celebrate the work of others via Twitter. Aside from when I'm promoting screenings of my film, I estimate that about 90 percent of my messages on Twitter are about articles and projects by other people, with just 10 percent or less about my own work. In my own experience, I don't like it so much when other people on Twitter or Facebook only talk about their own work. Collaboration and elevating each other are very important to me.

Put Down the Megaphone

For me, social networking platforms are simply an extension of physical spaces—those networking rooms or venues we frequently find ourselves in. LinkedIn is the office or industry conference. Facebook is the high school reunion or family gathering. Twitter is the cocktail party.

When I'm networking online, I remind myself to be the person other people want to talk to. Because here's the thing: networking on social platforms is not about one-way marketing; it's all about two-way interaction. It's a conversation, a dialogue. It's sharing information and ideas. It is most definitely not the equivalent of walking into a crowded party and announcing at the top of your lungs, "FRIENDS, I HAVE A BLACK FRIDAY 50 PERCENT OFF SALE!"

Ouch! Have I made you regret a recent tweet or post?

Good.

Because as IBM's Andrew Grill also likes to say, "I believe that social is just like real life."

Caution! There Are People behind That Platform

Social networking platforms are simply tools to be used selectively and with a whole lot of patience. The key to long-term social networking success is to always remember there are real people using the technology. People like you and me, with messy, complicated, distracted lives.

Tweeting in full caps is not the way to get their attention.

Platforms and apps inform all our social interactions, but what really drives networking is to focus on truly understanding who you are networking with. According to a Pew Research Center report on social media usage between 2005 and 2015, usage surged from 7 percent to 65 percent in only a decade.[28] While 90 percent of young adults are likely to be online and actively exploring new sites and platforms, the surge within established platforms (Facebook, LinkedIn) comes from those not-so-early adopters, older users. Social media usage by those sixty-five and older is now at 35 percent, compared to 2 percent a decade ago.

The first networking instinct of a millennial or gen Z may be to post, blog, or put a document in the cloud. And my guess is you're thinking the same cannot be said of a baby boomer or a member of the silent generation. But proceed with caution: there are increasingly fewer generational, racial, and gender differences when it comes to networking online. So if you need to network with an "older" person, you may want to skip the AARP meetup or scheduling a coffee at their office and friend the person on Facebook or send them a message on WhatsApp instead.

Working the Online Room

As a former lawyer, I used to joke that the greatest client-relations invention for the legal profession was voicemail. Many lawyers are introverts and prefer the company of a contract or legal brief to that of a client, colleague, or peer. With voicemail, lawyers could skip speaking with clients directly, let alone meeting with them. Then came e-mail, enabling the profession to retreat further from real human contact.

Technology is great, but it is too easy to hide behind the e-mail, voicemail, or texts; to skip a real, live interaction, convincing yourself that it's the right way to communicate essential information. A Facebook timeline full of personal updates blurs the passage of time between the moment when you liked the post and the last time you spent time with that person IRL, so use a post as a data point, not a substitute for a complete interaction.

I suspect we're far from the day when Slack replaces an all-hands meeting or an app effectively surfaces that replicates the subtle nuances of an initial business introduction. The point of technology may be to deliver information faster and seemingly more efficiently, but I'm primarily interested in making *effective* connections.

Use technology with the aim of getting offline, and always grab the chance to have an in-person meeting.

Hey! I Just Met You

I receive a fair number of "Hi, could you please add me to your LinkedIn connections?" messages from third-degree connections

I may have met at an event or second-degree connections who have been prompted to reach out because I fall into the "people you may know" category.

Hmm.

LinkedIn is an efficient way to stay connected and top-of-mind with recent introductions, former work colleagues, and new and ongoing business connections. It's my Rolodex (for those who remember what that is), my digital business-card, my business-relationship management system. It is all of the above! If it is work related, chances are I start my online research there.

But I'll admit it: my own business contact etiquette on the platform isn't perfect.

In some cases, it may be days or weeks after I've met someone at a conference or dinner or event that I finally find the time (or their business card in the bottom of my purse) to reach out. If "best practice" means sending an e-mail within twenty-four hours of meeting a new business contact, then my grade would be a pass, at best. And I know I'm not alone in not immediately sending the follow-up networking note.

This brings me back to the "standard" message LinkedIn provides when you invite someone to connect on that social networking site: "I'd like to add you to my professional network on LinkedIn."

Fifty-nine efficient little characters when combined together are not particularly helpful when you're busy, distracted, and scrambling to keep your head above the next wave of e-mails (as most of us are). If you're like me, and don't remember meeting someone (or the name of someone you did meet), this "standard" message causes unfortunate reactions like:

- That's nice, but who are you?
- How do I know you?
- Why do you want me to connect with you?

Standard "form" messages should be used with extreme care. Think of them as a suggestion only, then craft a personal note of introduction (or reintroduction). It may be efficient for you to use the standard message, but for the person you're sending the request to, your time saving is wasting their time.

When I receive a standard request with nothing more, I have to figure out:

- How I know you
- When we met
- Where we met
- Whether we said anything valuable
- Why we exchanged contact information
- Who we may have in common
- Why we may want to stay connected
- Whether you may be the person I remember talking to

You get the picture. I have to spend my time figuring out why you invited me to connect, rather than hitting the accept button and connecting with you. So, yes, when I see an auto-request with a name I don't readily recognize, I default to deleting the potential connection.

It makes it a lot easier to "accept" a request to connect when the person sending it includes context (for example, when we met, what we talked about, where the meeting was held, the color of your eyeglass frames, or what organization we both belonged to) and isn't simply saying, "Add me to your contacts."

The Water Cooler

One of Tina Roth Eisenberg's goals in designing her Friends coworking space was to create "water-cooler moments"—circumstances where conversations can lead to magical results. Water-cooler moments have led to Tina launching several of her businesses, so it is easy to understand why she's so passionate about cultivating this kind of serendipity.

What if you don't have a coworking space to go to every day or you're a digital nomad? Social networking platforms are where you seek those relationship-building, water-cooler moments. Water-cooler moments can happen on Slack or during a Twitter chat or from upvoting a product on Product Hunt. IBM's Andrew Grill creates not-entirely-left-to-chance interactions every time he travels—he refers to it as #socialserendipity.[29] Andrew makes it a point of mentioning where he's going, when he's arrived, and where he's staying (as well as looking for these cues from others in his global network). Andrew's role at IBM had him on the road for 114 days in 2015, so relying on social media to stay on top of his network as well as finding ways to start new conversations is an occupational necessity.

According to IBM, we're in the age of relationships and being social is not an option just for the extroverts in the workforce. It's an aspect of every role at IBM. Think about it! Why rely on a human resources team to recruit new talent when you can leverage the diverse experiences and talent of four hundred thousand employees? The same logic applies to business development too. By sending employees to social platforms as ambassadors for the brand, IBM is seeking those water-cooler moments where conversations can yield benefits—some real and some intangible. Without a doubt, IBM's network grows with every tweet, comment, and blog post by its four-hundred-thousand-strong networking team.[30]

Aim to create multiple touchpoints when creating your own online water-cooler moments. Here is a menu of more ideas to consider:

- If the person is an influencer, follow their posts on LinkedIn
- Sign up for their newsletter
- Write an Amazon review for their book
- Read and comment on their blog posts
- Subscribe to and spread the word about their podcasts—and rate their podcast on iTunes
- Share their content, whether by forwarding the insights to your friends via e-mail (or Facebook updates) or a post on LinkedIn or even simply a tweet or RT
- Remember to use their #hashtag
- Participate in a Twitter party they're hosting (or Q&A session hosted on the platform)
- Engage in their event(s) or meetups via Periscope or watch the live stream (many TEDx events do this)—and while you're virtually participating in the event share your insights on another platform (such as Twitter)

Searching for Work in Digital Spaces

Are you treating the Internet—and your network—as essential resources?

According the Pew Research Center, the Internet is an "essential employment resource" for today's job seekers.[31] During an employment search, we turn to the web as much as we do personal or professional networks. This is a pretty strong indication to me that you constantly need to have your online house in order. You may think you're digitally savvy, entrepreneurial, and outgoing; however, if your online interactions don't reflect that, who is going to believe you? Your online presence needs to work in unison with your offline ambitions. Google yourself if you need to verify this.

Look at Harriet Ruff, employee and brand advocate for IBM. Harriet had a strong external presence via her blog[32] and Twitter long before she was hired by IBM—and my guess is that it was her record, together with her hustle, that landed Harriet a coveted position at Big Blue. Harriet earned an English degree at college—a traditional résumé may have gotten her in the door, but her online activities took her career interests from there.

Expert Insights: Ask the Social Savvy Recruiter

"Posts frequently on weekends and while on airplanes" could be Amanda Ellis's eight-word biography. Amanda is vice president of search for Special Counsel. She is also a social media enthusiast who knows a lot about how to use social networking sites to get hired (she wrote *The 6Ps of the BIG 3™ for Job-Seeking JDs*, the first book to teach lawyers and law students how to get hired using social networking sites).

Amanda attributes her own network-building success online to:

■ Identifying and connecting with legal professionals on Twitter

■ Posting consistent content (that is: content related to the legal industry; her hometown of Dallas, or Texas; plus career-related topics and business travel)

■ Taking those conversations and connecting offline

Q: You're a social networking enthusiast who is also an executive recruiter, so you're uniquely positioned to advise professionals on how to approach social media. With respect to your own job in the highly competitive talent-recruitment market, what role does online connection play for you?

Amanda: I rely on Twitter, Facebook, and LinkedIn to gather insights and market intelligence about the legal industry. Specifically, I use the "list" feature on Twitter to monitor legal news across the United States. I use Facebook to see what lawyer friends are sharing about their firms and professional lives. And I use LinkedIn to gather a variety of professional updates and announcements. I'm an active participant on all three social networking sites—sharing information related to the legal industry as well as some of the internal job postings and positions we're recruiting for, on behalf of our clients. And, yes, our recruiters use LinkedIn Recruiter licenses to actively search for candidates.

Q: How does social media fit into your assessment of potential candidates? What do you look for? What are red flags? Is the absence of a digital footprint a problem? If so, why?

Amanda: Recruiters are fact checkers. A big red flag is a LinkedIn profile that doesn't match a corporate online bio or the CV that is attached to a potential candidate's e-mail. We work to place candidates in the right job, so Twitter feeds that consist only of automated content tweeted from your RSS feed (and no interaction with humans using Twitter) is poor signaling. Another note on the human element is to avoid sending generic LinkedIn invitations to people you haven't met. Taking a minute to tell me why you want to connect with me and how I can help you makes all the difference.

And, yes, the absence of a digital footprint needs to be explained. My first reaction is the person is hiding something! Most people, even those in regulated industries, are on at least one social networking site today.

Q: From content to connections, what's your advice on social media use for professionals looking to change careers or raise their visibility online?

Amanda: Here's a quick social to-do list I give job seekers:

- Maintain a polished, complete LinkedIn profile with a professional headshot.
- Post an update at least twice a week on LinkedIn for greater visibility. I recommend that your updates focus on industry-related news or an announcement about an event you are attending or a question posed to your network.
- Make an effort to Tweet at least five times a week. Tweets that are questions or comments to professionals in your industry are great ways to raise your visibility.
- Grow your network by connecting with everyone you meet on LinkedIn.

Q: You're a frequent business traveler. How do you approach maintaining all your connections? What tools and suggestions do you have?

Amanda: I rely on the location feature on LinkedIn. It sorts connections by geographic location—a gentle reminder about who you know and should reach out to when visiting a particular city. Again, the Twitter list feature is key for me, and I also use the Nuzzel app in case I don't have time to review my top two to three Twitter lists any given day when I'm on the road.

Q: You have a deep, industry-focused network. How have you gone about maintaining your professional connections?

Amanda: The short answer is being really diligent about maintaining my profile and consistency in the content I post. I've discovered that my network consists of many, many silent stalkers—that is, connections who are active consumers of social content but are not active content creators (or publicly liking or sharing content). I'll receive private messages from these people after posting content (just when I question whether anyone is reading it!), so I know that beyond a like or share, my consistent posting is being read.

What's Your Headline

Titles don't necessarily ignite conversation or reveal what you are capable of or striving for. Since we're all cobbling together careers based on the sum of our skills, interests, passion, and experience, why not share that as your tagline or headline or 140-character bio?

Which Networking Room Are You In?

When we think online networking, the default is more than likely to be the big three: LinkedIn, Twitter, Facebook. Of course, there's also Instagram, Snapchat, WhatsApp, and a host of other sites, from the social-content platform Medium to curated professional communities such as CreativeMornings and Levo.

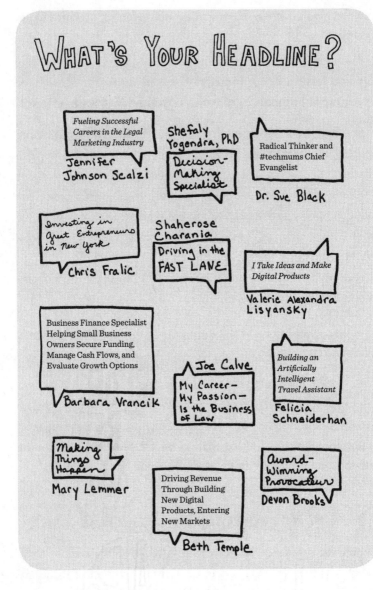

Now think again. Networking online means anywhere your name appears.

Take control and own this media! Don't let others define your online presence for you—or in your absence.

Working the online networking room also means paying close attention to how others exchange information on those platforms. The new networking rules in some ways mean there are no rules. For example, who said Instagram was just for pictures? Novelist Aidan Donnelley Rowley frequently uses her account[33] as a microblog and extension of the offline conversations she has at her Happier Hours literary salons. I use the "summary" box on LinkedIn as a way to keep my network informed on my upcoming speaking gigs or the conferences I'm attending. Did LinkedIn tell me I could do that? Nope. It just seemed to me to be a sensible way to use the tools it provided.

Networking online can also mean finding the information you need in new and novel venues. Why scroll through travel brochures for vacation inspiration when you can tap into a wanderlust community, starting first for inspiration on Instagram then moving to building a wish list on Airbnb, sourcing activities via Pinterest, then verifying travel plans socially with close friends on Snapchat and Facebook? This is exactly the networking route millennial traveler and IBM social business consultant Harriet Ruff took when planning a holiday in the Philippines[34]—and if you are a destination trying to attract millennial travelers, you should be worried if your social engagement strategy doesn't include a hashtag.

There's No Substitute for DIY

Etsy, the maker movement, DIY culture—I wish the enthusiasm for doing it or creating it yourself would creep back into the social networking space.

Unless you're the president of the United States or the mayor of New York City, you can't send someone else to attend a cocktail party for you. IMHO the same goes for social media. Sure, get someone to guide you as you create or edit your online profile. Definitely seek out help to understand whether you should use Hootsuite or Buffer or TweetDeck or another social media management tool. But then you need to take it from there. Social networking online is about being social and, yes, being social means interacting with other people. It's still networking— the cocktail party, conference, or reunion just happens to be taking place online.

Time in a Bottle

The autoresponse has become one of my signatures, much like my obsession with shoes. It is a strategic networking tactic plus an important time-management tool. We all have a love-hate relationship with e-mail. Yet for most of us, e-mail remains a key communication tool (shocker, it has not been replaced by Slack or Twitter or Instagram or Tumblr or LinkedIn or Facebook), and the autoresponder can be your productivity weapon too. I use it not only to inform or manage the expectations of people reaching out to contact me; I use it to manage myself.

If you're addicted to being hyperconnected 24-7, consider activating your e-mail autoresponse. The autoresponse prioritizes the time you actually spend in your e-mail inbox, providing the space you need to really focus on the people around you and projects to be completed.

Here are some other social time-management tactics to try out:

- Delete apps from your mobile device. For example, I do not have the LinkedIn or Facebook apps on my iPhone, and instead check these social platforms at scheduled times each day on my laptop.
- Limit the number of apps with access to cellular—it's less tempting without Wi-Fi.
- Turn off the biggest time waster of all—notifications from social media sites!

The reality is, the picture of your most recent meal (just like my shoe selfie) can wait.

There's an App for That

Every conference now has an app. At an invite-only investor event I attended in Cleveland, the conference organizer mentioned the event app and said their IT team was there to connect attendees so many times that I actually tuned out, doubting the sincerity of his promised ability to enable valuable connections. Conference planners and organizers often mistakenly believe that an app will facilitate not only the flow of logistical information (which session, which room, which keynote speaker) but also networking among the event attendees.

Don't underestimate the need for personal introductions or, worse, overvalue the role of an app as an effective substitute for connecting people. Technology is still a poor substitute for social engagement. Stop and think about it for a second: I suspect you've received a communication from someone (via e-mail, text, or instant messaging app) that has been, well, difficult to interpret. If we often miss nuances in real-life human relationships and find it difficult to read behind the social lines, why would we think technology, in the form of an app, will make it easier to interpret these subtle cues?

So get real (as in really human) when you're planning group interactions!

And besides, on a practical level, the value of an app depends entirely on the people using it—from whether they have downloaded the app at all to whether they have bothered to complete a profile.

An app, like a social networking site, is just one of many tools you'll use to engage with other people. Digital is the newer, perhaps more serendipitous version of in-person networking. However, it is a fallacy to think it completely replaces the need for old-school exchange-of-business-cards networking. The fact remains that simple human interaction has proven difficult to automate.

Plan your networking approach so it works for people, not algorithms.

6

Connecting the Dots

IN OUR HYPERCONNECTED world, how you let people know what you know—or what you need, want, or desire—becomes key. And you do that by constantly connecting the dots between your goals and the ways your network can help you.

No, not by randomly tossing out e-mails or posts on social media with high hopes and little thought! Rather, by being intentional about how and when you tap into your network. It's all about being considerate in the ways you go about asking for help. It's not assuming, and it is definitely not keeping your network guessing about what you need or what you're up to.

By linking the networking dots, you become a connector. Not a connector in the way Malcolm Gladwell describes them in his book *The Tipping Point*[35] (that is, by knowing lots of people and being in the habit of making introductions). Imagine yourself more like a quarterback with an eye on the ultimate goal and strategizing each connecting pass and play to get there. Become that type of connector for your career. Because when you connect your goals to the right contacts across all your networks (educational, cultural, social, geographic, professional, economic, religious, and political), your network will be powerfully positioned to help you.

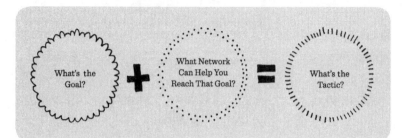

Make the Connection: Career Change

My success in navigating a career change back in 2002 to 2004 came (as you've learned) from support within my network, never from a help-wanted ad. It also came about from knowing exactly what I wanted to achieve (information or an introduction). By keeping a clear picture in my mind of the role I was after, I knew who in my network to turn to for help. And, no, I didn't ask everyone for help.

Before you hit Send on the generic "I need a new job" e-mail to all your friends or reach for your mobile to send a job-search SOS, ask yourself, "What is my career goal?" Is it simply earning a paycheck? Is it a challenging role on Wall Street or getting a foot in the door with a hot Silicon Valley startup? Is it finding work with meaning or learning from a visionary CEO?

You may be fortunate enough to have lots of connections who can help you "get a job," but ask yourself, Who should you be connecting with to get the job or launch the career you really want?

You also want to narrowly define what you're seeking before you start networking to make it happen. Announcing that you "need a job" is asking a question that's too hard for your network to answer. The need is too vague and requires clarification: Are you looking for something full time or part time? Would you consider freelance or remote work? Do you want a job like the one you had before? Will you relocate? Whoa! By broadcasting that need, you're asking your network to take on your job research, not just aid you in your job search. A generic ask is an exhausting task for your network.

The networking takeaway: Time is a limited resource, so seek other people's time wisely. For example, you don't want to waste someone's time (and your chance to make a valuable career connection) with general background questions in an informational interview. By doing your research in advance, you will be prepared to ask more detailed, specific questions that will gain you valuable insight. Another networking given is to follow up. Send the thank-you note. Check in periodically to let the person you've met with know how your job search is progressing. If they've made an introduction, be sure to let them know how that meeting went too. And take another look at Jessica Peltz-Zatulove's interview in chapter 3 if you need a refresher!

3 QUESTIONS

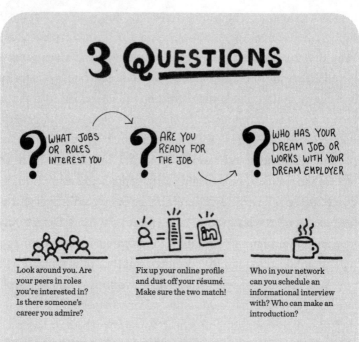

WHAT JOBS OR ROLES INTEREST YOU

ARE YOU READY FOR THE JOB

WHO HAS YOUR DREAM JOB OR WORKS WITH YOUR DREAM EMPLOYER

Look around you. Are your peers in roles you're interested in? Is there someone's career you admire?

Fix up your online profile and dust off your résumé. Make sure the two match!

Who in your network can you schedule an informational interview with? Who can make an introduction?

Be curious! What are your career possibilities? Use LinkedIn and other social platforms to research roles you're interested in *(and the desired educational background or skills needed in order to be successful).*

Are there other skills you need to acquire? Leap over the "no experience" hurdle by learning those job skills before you're on the job. Classes and courses are also networking opportunities for landing that next job.

Informational interviews provide job search clarity and can lead to further introductions (as well as job leads).

Understand what you're looking for and what you need to do to get there.

Be specific when you ask for someone's time! What is it you want to learn from them?

Make the Connection: Media and PR

Wealth management advisor Manisha Thakor is active in traditional and print media, as she understands that being quoted or interviewed on air keeps her top-of-mind with existing and potential clients (her business networking story appears in chapter 2). Manisha has also cultivated a relationship with journalists covering personal finance stories. She makes a point of being as helpful as possible, whether by providing insights, returning inquiries promptly, or recommending other qualified experts. Manisha also continually positions herself to be found on the basis of her expertise, both in the content she produces (i.e., regular newsletters) and by taking a point-of-view approach to posting updates on LinkedIn. All of this makes her expertise easy to find—which is helpful for the media too.

You may be thinking, so what? *The New York Times* has been upended by BuzzFeed, and Snapchat is more likely to break the news to millennials than *The Washington Post* or CNN. While it is absolutely true that the media is being upended by digital technology and social networks, traditional media (print, TV, and radio) still retain massive power to launch careers and products. Entrepreneurs and executives alike continue to be interested in knowing how they can be quoted or featured, as that press is usually part of the connected equation for where they want to be next.

A typical question that lands in my e-mail runs along these lines: "My friends have just launched their product on Kickstarter. Do you know anyone who might want to cover it?"

That's too vague and too big a question to ask your network. By asking that kind of question, what you're really asking your network to do is to tell your story, find your media angle, and source the outlets to publish it. You need to give your contacts more specific information to enlist their help in attracting media attention!

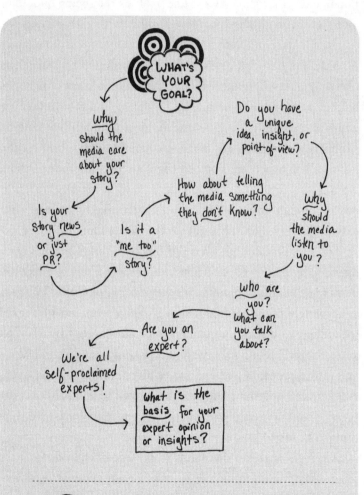

WHAT'S YOUR GOAL?

Why should the media care about your story?

Do you have a unique idea, insight, or point-of-view?

How about telling the media something they don't know?

Is your story news or just PR?

Is it a "me too" story?

Why should the media listen to you?

Who are you? What can you talk about?

Are you an expert?

We're all self-proclaimed experts!

What is the basis for your expert opinion or insights?

By answering the tough questions first, you're better positioned to get help from your network (than would otherwise come from tossing out a vague *"do you know anyone who might want to"* and crossing your fingers).

A good story with the expertise to back it up gets media attention. Your goal defines your strategy for pitching the story. Because the reality is, not every news outlet cares about your product launch or crowdfunding project. But someone might. Someone might really want to tell your story—and it is *your* job

Which publications, journalists, and media sources are you going to pitch? What's the best way to reach them (*Twitter or e-mail or personal introduction*)?

Got a **STORY** and the street cred to back it up? **GREAT!**

Is your story **PR**, not new news? Can't find an expert reason for the media to talk to you (yet)?

Save the networking ask for now by spending your time researching the issues (what's the story that is not being told?) and/or establishing why you're the "go-to" on this subject (*tip: spruce up your LinkedIn profile by listing awards and recent media or speaking engagements*).

to figure out who! Why does the media want to hear about you? This is a standard networking "think about the other person" (the journalist, media outlet, their audience) scenario!

Answer that question before you start drafting outreach e-mails to your contacts. It is not likely that your goal is simply to get your name in print or a mention in a blog. Are you looking to become the next Oprah or increase sales or announce a new service or round of funding? What's the goal? What's the reason you want media attention and press mentions for your initiative, product, service, or vision?

The networking takeaway: You want the journalist to tell your story, so be the great go-to news source! Follow journalists on Twitter[36] and retweet their stories. If they're looking for sources, provide them with recommendations. Be as genuinely interested in helping them do their job as you want them to be in helping you! And don't be shy with your expertise. Share your opinions in your updates on LinkedIn or posts on Medium. Be sure your online profile is up to date and includes the factual foundation for why you're really an expert.

Make the Connection: Crowdfunding

A successful crowdfunding effort requires more than a dream and a sharp video. As Kathryn Finney's story in chapter 3 illustrates, it requires having and tapping into a network. The necessity of having and using a network is often poorly planned or sadly overlooked in crowdfunding efforts.

In the final week of their crowdfunding campaign, the founders of a social-commerce company e-mailed me. The startup,

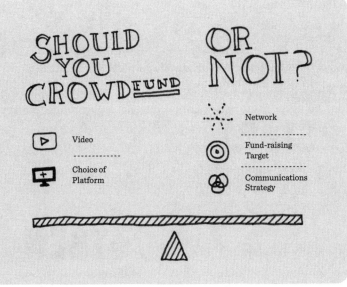

founded by Ivy League college classmates, focused on bringing chic, ethically made ready-to-wear products to market. The founders decided to crowdfund the ten thousand dollars they needed to produce the first collection, made from artisan-designed fabrics. They were falling short of their funding target and in desperation had begun to reach out to complete strangers for help (and money).

I had a nagging suspicion from the start of the call that this startup had not done everything it could to connect its existing networks to its fund-raising efforts. There is a saying in the startup community: when you ask for money, you get advice, and if you ask for advice, you get money. You know where this is headed. As much as, I'm sure, they appreciated my advice, these founders were really seeking a donation—sprinkled with

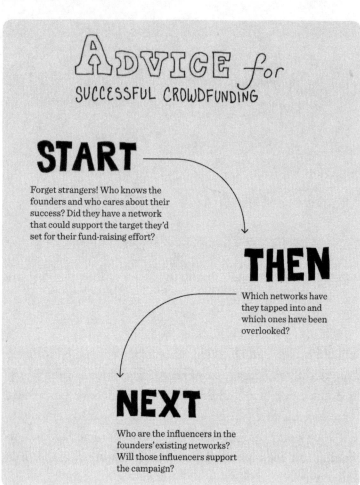

ADVICE *for*
SUCCESSFUL CROWDFUNDING

START

Forget strangers! Who knows the
founders and who cares about their
success? Did they have a network
that could support the target they'd
set for their fund-raising effort?

THEN

Which networks have
they tapped into and
which ones have been
overlooked?

NEXT

Who are the influencers in the
founders' existing networks?
Will those influencers support
the campaign?

a little social influence. Above is the advice I gave them to get
their crowdfunding effort over the funding-success line (they
ultimately raised the ten thousand dollars they needed from
thirty-two funders).

I quickly concluded that this founding team was not lacking in networks to tap into: the core team consisted of six peo-

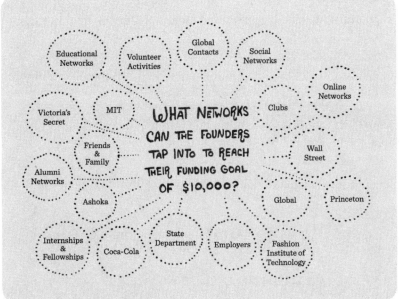

ple with professional experience in fashion, higher education, banking, not-for-profit, and tech startups. The key to fundraising success is to ask and activate existing networks. The primary purpose of a crowdfunding platform (whether it is Kickstarter, Indiegogo, GoFundMe, or any of the other thousands of sites out there) is simply to facilitate payments! The platform is not responsible for sourcing funders or marketing a campaign to the project's network; the person with the project must do that.

These founders had overlooked the large, diverse existing network they already had. To reach their funding goal, they simply had to communicate their need to their existing network! Ultimately, the challenge in the remaining days of the crowdfunding campaign was to come up with a three-part communications strategy to quickly reach a wider network of potential funders/donors sourced exclusively from within their existing network:

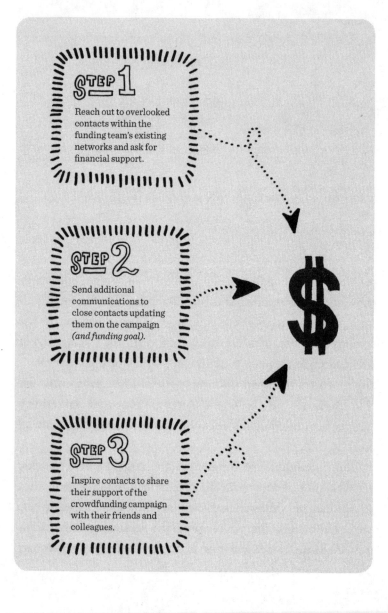

STEP 1
Reach out to overlooked contacts within the funding team's existing networks and ask for financial support.

STEP 2
Send additional communications to close contacts updating them on the campaign *(and funding goal).*

STEP 3
Inspire contacts to share their support of the crowdfunding campaign with their friends and colleagues.

Crowdfunding is an example (again) of how people in your network can help you reach a goal and how by focusing solely on the functionality of a tool or promise of technology you risk missing out on an achievable goal!

If you're considering a crowdfunding campaign:

- Remember that your success depends on mobilizing support from people who already know you.
- Before you start planning your campaign, brainstorm and list all possible networks you can turn to for financial support.
- Put your ego aside (you're asking for money after all!) and be prepared to reach deep into your networks for help.
- Get creative about how you can activate those weak connections (i.e., the second cousin you haven't talked to since the last family reunion or the boss from your job two summers ago).
- Plan a thirty-day communications strategy—not just a day-of-launch strategy. Think of multiple ways to update your network (e-mail, calls, Facebook posts) to keep them involved and supportive of your crowdfunding effort.
- Plan a postcampaign strategy too, as completing a crowdfunding campaign is just the first of many challenges your project will face. Keep this energized community active with ongoing updates about your efforts.
- On a practical note, if you're building a lifestyle brand, realize it takes a lot of content and a whole lot of community—and a lot longer than a thirty-day crowdfunding campaign—to captivate new hearts and minds. If you only have thirty days, then reach deep into the network of people who already know and believe in you!

PREPARATION for CROWDFUNDING

Who knows you and will support your crowdfunding campaign?

Make a list of all your networks!

If you ask your network for money, how much could you raise?

Think about surveying your network before you finalize details (such as donation levels + rewards).

Plan the communications strategy for your campaign. Who do you need to get on board first?

Set your crowdfunding target based on what you know your network will give + a stretch goal.

Enlist the support of enthusiasts in your network.

Which communications tools work best with your network?

What networks have you overlooked?

The networking takeaway: Throughout your campaign, acknowledge the support you've received from people in your network. Reach out to them individually and personally (whether it is a call, a handwritten note sent in the post, or personalized electronic note sent using Red Stamp or Paperless Post). Don't leave the community cold once your crowdfunding campaign is over!

Send periodic updates on your progress—after all, these people believed in you enough to rally behind your fund-raising effort.

Make the Connection: Startup or New Business Communications

Everyone reaches out for help just when they need it—and expects their network to immediately jump into action. Enough of the 911 networking calls! This is often the easiest networking challenge to prevent (not just solve) and the one most entrepreneurs and small business owners have trouble doing, let alone getting right. Your need for an introduction to an investor or for a social media post in support of a Mother's Day marketing campaign does not need to become a networking emergency. All it takes is communicating regularly with your network—plus a little persistence and planning.

Regular and steady communications—before you need the help—win the race. I know, being preached about consistency in networking activities is as enticing as ten more sit-ups, but don't just take my word for it that the consistent, concise e-mail-update approach pays off: New York City based startup Hitlist reached two hundred thousand initial downloads of its travel app on the iTunes Store with no marketing costs simply by sending a weekly e-mail to people in its network.[37]

Regular communications connect your friends, family, advisors, mentors, and potential investors to your journey as a startup founder or new business owner. From the start, these are the people who know you and want to see you succeed. Keep them close during your journey and they'll truly be invested in your success. That new problem you're facing? Chances are someone in your network (or someone who knows someone) can provide an answer. That information you wanted shared on Twitter? I'm pretty sure they'll jump on helping you with that too.

The new economy may be real time and on demand; rela-

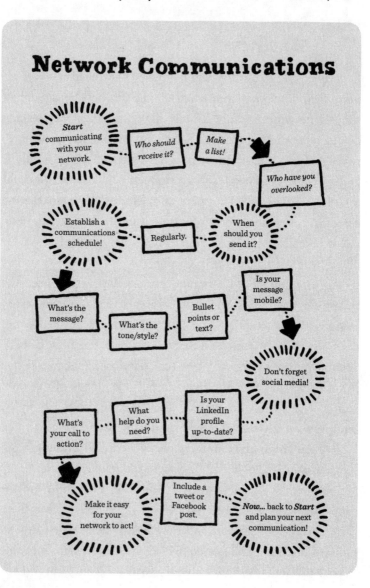

tionships, however, are not. Communicate regularly and thoughtfully so your network can help you.

- Where to start? Brainstorm a contact list. This is a list of
  all the people you should be sharing your business highs
  and lows with.
- Create an e-mail list or customized list on MailChimp. A
  Google+ circle may work equally well for you (or perhaps a
  private group on LinkedIn or closed group on Facebook).
  Your list may fit nicely on a spreadsheet, or maybe connecting the list to tasks by using one of the many interactive
  platforms (Trello, Slack, Basecamp, Podio, or Asana) suits
  your project and/or time-management style. The point is
  to spend some time thinking about who should be on your
  list, then assemble all that contact information on a platform or tool you'll use.
- If you're wondering when you should send out a communication to your network, I hate to tell you that the only
  person who can answer that question is . . . you. Not e-mail
  marketing data or looking at what your competitor does.
  Only you can decide the timing and frequency of communications. Think about the people in your network and
  what time of day is best for them to receive your message.
- Once you've decided when to send your update (weekly,
  monthly, on Tuesday afternoons, whatever!) stick to that
  timing, regardless of how exhausted or stressed or deadline driven you are. It's hard and it takes commitment—I
  know, I've been there! In February 2015 I committed to
  sending out a weekly e-mail called *Innovator Insights*, to
  grow my network. There were weeks when I stared at the
  computer screen wondering if I had anything to say (and if

anyone was even reading my newsletter). I know I'll have those weeks again. You'll realize, as I have, that over time your network has an expectation of hearing from you. And knowing this (plus understanding the value that comes from keeping it informed) will motivate you to draft the next newsletter or e-mail update and the one after that.

- Remind yourself constantly that networks determine which ideas become breakthroughs or get funding, media mentions, vital connections, etc. Keep your network informed so your ideas have a bigger audience to lean on.

- Wondering what to say? Craft a message that makes it easy for the recipients to want to help you. Always keep in mind that behind every e-mail address is a human being with a messy, complicated life (and their own urgencies and priorities). Balance your need with the aim of educating, informing, or delighting your audience.

- Don't forget to imagine where the people in your network are actually reading your message—are they commuting to work or at home in the evening? Are they reading it on an iPhone, iPad, or laptop? It may be your message, but it's their time you've asked for, so make it worthwhile and put it in a format they will actually read.

- Sharing spreads your ideas further, so don't overlook posting business updates on social media. If someone misses your e-mail, they may pay attention to your Facebook post. A new business contact may be checking your LinkedIn updates.

The networking takeaway: The trust and respect you build with your contacts grows stronger over time, especially when you show that you value their time—as well as their guidance. By sweating the small, regular communications, people really get to know you (and in an overloaded, always-on world, you want to be the message they trust and look forward to receiving).

Make the Connection: From Vision Board to TEDx Stage

You met Varelie Croes in chapter 4. Her career path—tax associate to tax manager to director of international tax financial services—does not sound like the topic for a TEDx talk, but guess what? Varelie has been on the TEDx stage twice. Her ambition to speak at TEDx started on a vision board then with help from her network became a reality.

After eleven years at PwC, Varelie took advantage of a generous paid-leave benefit the firm offered to all director-level executives. Viewing the six weeks off as an opportunity to assess her career direction and to set future professional goals, Varelie handed over her BlackBerry and deactivated her PwC e-mail.

During her sabbatical, Varelie started a journal, read extensively, and reconnected with her values. She also watched a lot of TED Talks and discovered "Start with Why" by Simon Sinek. Listening to Simon's story, Varelie imagined sharing her own story and inspiring people to action.

Varelie returned to work in September 2013 and quickly slipped back into her hectic 24-7 work routine, with one change: she joined a mastermind group for women entrepreneurs. Varelie realized during her sabbatical that her core network was composed of executives and professionals in the financial, legal, and professional-services industries. A great network to continue her advancement at PwC but not to help her make a significant career shift. She also realized she needed a support group to call upon—especially one that was enthusiastically pursuing their career choices, regardless of the challenges! Varelie selected a mastermind group made up of entrepreneurs, in order to get a fresh look at (plus candid feedback on) her big ideas.

At one of her mastermind group's weekend retreats, Varelie met Alexia Vernon, founder of Influencer Academy and a coach who specializes in helping executives develop TED-worthy presentations. Alexia's message to Varelie was simple: you need to tell your story and do a TED Talk one day.

After the meeting, Varelie did the digital follow-up: she connected with Alexia on Facebook.

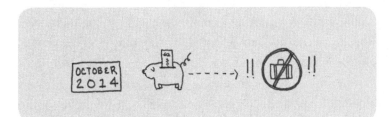

A year after taking her six-week sabbatical and aggressively saving her paychecks, Varelie pulled the trigger and quit her job.

Home for the holidays, Varelie picked up the book *How to Deliver a TED Talk,* as she was still harboring thoughts about giving a TED Talk one far-off day in the future. During her vacation, she also began watching tons of TED Talks and created a vision board.

Back in New York and randomly checking her social networking accounts, Varelie noted a post from Alexia circulating the dates of upcoming TEDxWomen events. Curious, Varelie browsed the list and discovered and event had been scheduled in Aruba. Not one to wait to be asked, Varelie put the word out to her network in Aruba that she was interested in presenting at the event. To maximize her chances of being considered, Varelie updated her online bio, citing noteworthy events she'd spoken at as well as articles she'd published and any media mentions.

As a result of her updated LinkedIn profile (edits to her profile were spotted by a friend scouting speakers for a Global Shakers & Makers event), Varelie was invited to speak at the World Bank. It was the perfect opportunity to outline her career story and test the content she was considering for a TED Talk.

Varelie's network spread the word, and two months after spotting the Facebook post, the TEDxWomen (Aruba) organizer called Varelie to set up a meeting. At the "get to know you" meeting, Varelie was asked to speak at the event. In spite of having less than a month to prepare her remarks, Varelie jumped at the opportunity.

With the help of her mastermind group (and coaching from her friend Alexia), five months after starting her TED vision board, Varelie delivered her first TEDx Talk. The event was live-streamed globally, with her name appearing on the global TEDx Women agenda next to speakers such as Billie Jean King and Jimmy Carter. Beyond a laser focus on delivering a powerful talk, Varelie made networking at the event a priority, as she knew the organizers of upcoming TEDxAruba were there scouting speakers for their larger and higher-profile event.

Varelie's TEDxWomen was a success (she was voted audience favorite) and as a result she was invited to speak at TEDx-Aruba.

Knowing she could make no mistakes onstage at TEDx-Aruba (the talks were live-streamed to all the Dutch embassies globally), Varelie locked herself in a hotel room the day before the event and practiced as if her life depended on it! Varelie delivered her TEDxAruba talk, and her remarks spiraled into more invitations and speaking opportunities.

The networking takeaway:

- Assess your current network. You may need to seek out a new, expanded network to help you reach your future goals.
- You're living in an era where it is not who you know or what you know; rather, it's who knows what you know! Regularly sharing your goals with your network is an essential activity!
- Prepare and put yourself in front of opportunities by keeping your social profiles up to date and monitoring the content your network is posting.

Connecting Your Goal, Purpose, and Connections

Now it's your turn! Time to get those big ideas and ambitions out of your head and to plan the path to connect them with your network. Whether you doodle on the side of a notebook or grab a bunch of Post-it notes along with a Sharpie or use the sample goal work sheet, get specific about what you're seeking to achieve and actively focus on who in your network can help you reach your goals.

WHAT MAKES YOU *different?*

What is driving you to pursue this goal?

WHAT ARE YOU TRYING TO DO?

Your goal:

Get your ideas out of your head and out to your network!

WHO HAVE YOU TALKED TO ABOUT YOUR GOAL?

Who needs your skills? Insights? Product? Service? Point-of-view? Expertise?

WHO ELSE?

What actions are you taking to achieve it?

WHY DOES THIS GOAL MATTER?

WHAT ELSE?

WHAT WILL YOU DO NEXT TO ACHIEVE YOUR GOAL?

7

Networking #Fail

SUNDAY NIGHTS I try to adhere to a "get ready for the week" routine. This means I have the best intentions to review my calendar for the coming week, scan e-mails, and add any new tasks to my TeuxDeux list. In doing so one night, I came across a message on LinkedIn from a former colleague. He mentioned that it had been a while since we'd chatted and that recently he had been asked to chair a committee. If I was still in New York City, he would like to seek my advice over coffee.

Ugh. My Sunday night routine quickly soured. The sender was absolutely correct; it had been a while since we'd last chatted: seven years, to be correct. The rapport we'd had vaporized not with time but because he seemed not to have bothered to quickly glance over my profile to see what I'd been up to since exiting the nine-to-five of Monday to Friday. And, yes, my profile quite clearly indicates that I'm still based in New York City. I realize it is a networking fail not to keep an online profile up to date. It is equally a failure not to review an online profile, with some attention to detail, in advance of reaching out.

The subsequent exchange over LinkedIn was a time-wasting back-and-forth until my former colleague finally asked a direct question about the information he was really seeking, and then, only then, could I provide the helpful answer. Unfortunately, during the communication process the cozy warmth of former-colleague rapport rapidly vaporized.

Nothing like a networking fail to start the week.

Locked Doors and Blocked Paths

In tech entrepreneur and academic Vivek Wadhwa's October 2014 *Washington Post* editorial, "The Glaring Gender Dilemma Silicon Valley Venture Capitalists Are Hiding From,"[38] one line really stood out for me: "He insisted that I would never be able to make the right connections to be successful in the valley."

The ability to make connections is essential in the innovation economy, particularly in its global heart, Silicon Valley. The importance of connections in the tremendous effort it takes to launch and scale a company, let alone to become a member of the elite 1 percent club (only 1 percent of US businesses receive venture-capital funding), is also mentioned briefly in the study cited by Wadhwa in his column: "Nonetheless, women were consistently left out of the networks of growth capital finance and appeared to lack the contacts needed to break through."

As I mentioned back at the very start of this book, opportunities have presented themselves to me as a result of this career cocktail:

Expertise + professional objective + network of contacts

Who I knew opened doors for me at critical junctures in my career. It altered not only my career path but also my perspective on what I could be and, more important, how I had the power to do the same for someone else. Access changes everything.

I am continually perplexed by a networking mind-set that chooses to close doors, to keep the club small, to limit opportunity. It is a networking failure in generosity, to say the very least. You're bound to encounter these types, so here are some suggestions about how to minimize their impact on your pursuit of a goal:

- End the meeting politely. There is no point in continuing a painfully unproductive discussion.
- This may appear counterintuitive; however, don't skip the follow-up just because it was an unpleasant first encounter. The person may have been unsupportive in that moment, but you never know down the road. And, heck, you may have just caught them on a particularly bad day.
- Check in periodically via e-mail to keep the person informed about your progress. Don't ask for anything or anticipate a response; simply send them your latest news. And don't worry: if the person doesn't want to hear from you again, they will definitely let you know.
- Spend a little time decoding why you wanted to meet this person. Were your expectations for the outcome of the meeting in line with what your meeting preparation (or gut) was telling you? Sometimes the enthusiasm of securing a meeting with an influencer trumps our networking common sense—and you don't want to constantly make this mistake.

Death Eaters

If you're not a Harry Potter fan, too bad. You're not excused from this networking point.

In the Potter books, Death Eaters are evil witches and wizards. In networking parlance, they are the people who constantly ask for help or new connections or random introductions but who never, ever reciprocate in kind. No thanks or consideration, just endless asks. Masters of thinking only about what *they* need, Death Eaters are the people who zap your energy and kill the strength of your connections.

Avoid them. And, more important, follow the networking guidance in this book to avoid becoming one.

Intruders

You are the gatekeeper to your own network. Manage the introductions you choose to make, to ensure success. The person you are introducing may only need your prized contact once—you likely need that contact for a lifetime.

Who have you helped recently? is the question Evan Nisselson wants answered before he makes an introduction for someone in his network. As Evan shared in chapter 1, he has adopted a Silicon Valley give-forward mentality and willingly shares his connections with those who live by the same networking philosophy. My gatekeeper's approach is a little more New York and direct—I need to know why you want an introduction, and why the introduction benefits the other person, before I'll invade an inbox or overburden my contacts with another request. You need to find a style that works for you and safeguards your network.

Hey! I Just Met You (Remix)

The biggest networking waste of time is to waste other people's time, especially when the information is readily available elsewhere. Not doing the research is not being a generous networker. Making big, unfocused networking asks is another networking annoyance. Make it easy for your network to help you.

Evan Nisselson frequently receives "I'm coming to NYC— who should I meet?" e-mails from far-flung corners of his network. This is a big pain of a question because the person being asked doesn't know where to start in answering it! This is not the way to ask for help via an introduction or connection. Instead, specify your goals (e.g., "I'm looking to set up business-development meetings with media companies") and how the person you're connected to can help ("And I see you're connected to X, Y, Z on LinkedIn. Do you know them well enough to make an introduction?"). This may seem like common sense, but, not so amusingly, people get this wrong all the time.

Avoiding 911

I'm a broken record on the subject of avoidable networking emergencies. As I frequently respond to startup founders who approach me with questions about funding: your friends, fans, and followers won't turn on a dime to help you unless you bring them along on your journey.

Networking is connecting through sharing stories and experiences. It's building a human connection, not simply stating a need to be filled (or, in the case of startups, a check to be written). An urgent need for an introduction to an investor, a contribution to a future crowdfunding campaign, or a post on social media to support a Valentine's Day marketing campaign does not need to become an emergency. It is a communications failure. It is avoidable. You fail at networking when you don't take steps to communicate your dreams, ambitions, and goals regularly to friends, family, advisors, mentors, and/or potential investors.

Regular communications are the signposts on your career journey, so bring your friends, family, advisors, mentors, and investors along on that journey with you! By keeping them engaged, you build rapport and trust rather than diminishing it with an e-mail or Facebook post seeking last-minute assistance.

That insurmountable problem you're facing? Chances are you're not the first to face it, and likely there is someone in your network (or someone who knows someone) who can provide guidance. This is free, experienced, informed guidance that would have happily been delivered up in an e-mail, call, or coffee date if you had simply shared your progress and not just the great challenge you're "suddenly" facing. Guidance that, had it been given along the way, well before you made that hiring decision or applied for that job, could have saved you a whole lot of time, energy, and money—the resources you have in very short supply.

Another upside to not being that 911 networker? If they feel regularly connected to your efforts, your network will only become more vocal supporters and champions of them.

Keep Your Qualifications Connected

Here is another reason not to sit quietly on the digital sidelines until you need help with something such as landing a new job.

In the course of writing this book, a job opening for a Google BrandLab media and product strategist caught my eye (it popped up in my stream of LinkedIn updates). I found this job opening interesting, not because of the frequency with which it recurred in my digital network, but rather because of Google's approach to recruiting. Yes, having connections within an organization has always helped one land an interview, but now that reality is completely out in the open—valued, suggested, and of merit. In this case, right next to Google's big red Apply Now button was an equally prominent Find Connections search box followed by the tag, "Know someone at Google? Reach out to them." To drive home the point that Google values job candidates referred by Google employees, there was also a bright Google-blue banner across the top saying, "Hi there! We can use your Google+ profile information to help you find relevant jobs and connections at Google." The message is clear: the new way to search for a job is digitally driven and fueled by having connections.

An inside track through a personal recommendation is one way to land a job (and a motivation to complete your online profile and to keep it up to date). This is also the upside of using the digital tools at hand and staying loosely connected to a broad network on social media!

Dropping the Ball

Another networking fail—and the flip side to waiting until you have a massive, urgent need to reach out to your contacts—is only reaching out when you discover that someone you used to know has landed a big, new job or coveted role or some other desired claim to fame. I'm not going to discourage you from sending a congratulatory handwritten note (or e-mail or Facebook post); however, I'll temper your expectations: don't expect much enthusiasm in return. I'm not being cynical, just practical. Your networking silence is a bigger indication of how much you value someone than a congratulatory note that arrives after the headlines and hard work. It's often just a little too little, a little too late. It smacks of saying, "Now that you're a success you're useful to me."

One of my fellow board members at a New York City not-for-profit went to law school with a former US president. It was clear, according to the board member, that his law-school classmate was destined for greatness. A poll of the class would have verified this, so in many ways it was no surprise when his former classmate was elected to the top office. The networking fail? This board member, in spite of the rapport and admiration for his classmate, had never stayed in touch. Not a holiday card. Not a "well done!" note until the classmate made it to the Oval Office (and there had been plenty of alumni network opportunities for "good job!" communications between graduation and Election Day). The polite standard form response he received on White House embossed letterhead—and the lesson that staying in touch is good networking—are the only upsides to this story.

Keep that in mind as you leave school and switch jobs. Don't cut off the connections—your story about the number of times you played foosball with the future president of the United States is a little less impressive when someone discovers you never made any effort to stay in touch.

The Dump and Drive

To say I am not a fan of the "you two should know each other" e-mail is an understatement. I refer to these sorts of e-mails as "dump and drive." Someone with seemingly good intentions thinks two people should meet, sends an e-mail with no further information, and whizzes off. Dropped in someone's e-mail inbox without context (or permission), this sort of message typically leaves recipients cold to the introduction because they are left to figure out *why* the introduction was even made. Figuring out the reason for your unsolicited introduction is work—and not networking work your contacts want to take on. It's your job to explain why!

When someone who is ridiculously busy takes the time to write a blog post on the "drive and dump" e-mail, you know this is a very serious networking fail indeed! Back in March 2013, First Round Capital's Chris Fralic wrote a post for Forbes.com on the topic of e-mailing busy people (like venture partners). I still refer people to Chris's timeless post, "The Art of the Email Introduction: 10 Rules for Emailing Busy People."[39] As Chris states in rule 1, "The Ask":

> Sometimes it makes sense to just make the introduction when asked, but in most cases I think it's a best practice to ask for and receive permission before an introduction is made. This makes it a choice for the recipient and doesn't create an obligation.

Adventurer Alison Levine is equally adamant about this networking taboo. Her biggest networking tip is never, and she means *never*, make a "blind introduction" to someone. Always ask their permission first, and give them detail and background about *why* you are making the introduction.

You may think you are making a helpful networking introduction or connection; however, without the ask, your e-mail (regardless of the level of detail it contains) may have inadvertently inconvenienced or annoyed one or more of the recipients, and suddenly your valued direct e-mail line to an important contact could be short-circuited as a result of one well-intentioned but poorly planned e-mail.

Oversharing

I'm a highlighter. When it comes to sharing personal information online, I typically only offer upbeat, positive news.

According to some friends who are more active and savvy online than I am, this is a networking fail. Okay, I *could* share a little more online than stories of my shoe obsession or work travel or career advice, but my attitude is, does anyone really want to know the intimate details of my daily life, from the dull to the routine to the anxiety causing? I'm not a performance artist, so I don't feel my whole life needs to be on display. I'm selective and share what I think is the good stuff. However, based on the feedback I've received, I'm rethinking what I post to ensure there is balance. What we're all seeking online is a stronger bond, and if displaying all sides of our lives (from the good to the bad) instills greater trust and connection, I'm all for modifying the way I choose to post.

Sharing too much can be a networking fail just as much as sharing too little. Only you can determine if your network cares about what you ate for lunch (are you a foodie, a cook, or a diabetic?) but rethink rants on Facebook about how much you hate your job or why venture capitalists suck. When personal recommendations mean access, who wants to risk their reputation by recommending a constant complainer for a new position, internship, promotion, or funding?

You live by your communications—and can get skewered by them too! So think before you post—and, oh yeah, check your privacy settings while you're at it.

Passing without Passing Off

A tip I learned from an executive recruiter: always take the call. What does that mean exactly?

If a recruiter calls you, take his or her call, even if it's for an opportunity you're not interested in, not qualified for, or don't think you're ready to pursue. Don't ignore the call simply because the timing is off or the opportunity isn't what you're currently looking for! That call from the recruiter is your chance to network your future—to tell the recruiter about your career ambitions and about the next opportunity you'd like. Recruiters do, after all, talk and network with one another.

When I was still working in law-firm management, I used to have lunch once a year with an executive recruiter in the industry. When we first met, it was too early for her to place me in a role (I did not have enough "real" experience), but she believed in me and was willing to help as a sounding board or to refer leads. A strong professional relationship developed from there. Annually, she gave me insights into roles, department budgets, and salaries at competitor firms—vital information as I negotiated on my behalf and, ultimately, on behalf of my staff. Had I stayed in the profession, there is no doubt I would have turned to her for help landing my next role, because after four years of networking, I knew I had a powerful advocate in the industry.

Beyond your own future ambitions, here's another reason to take the recruiter's call: that job that is "not for you" may be just the thing for someone in your network and you'll be helping out both of them by making the connection. And you never know down the road when you'll need two more champions in your career corner.

Following without Following Up

Introductions and conversations over breakfast or cocktails are lost opportunities without the follow-up note, call, or e-mail. The enthusiasm of the conversation evaporates as time passes. We all know this, so why is the follow-up—which is likely the most effective networking tool—so often neglected? After she makes an introduction, adventurer Alison Levine always tells people, "Let me know how it goes, after you meet." She inserts the expectation of a follow-up as a consideration for making the introduction, because she wants to know how things turn out. She wants to know if the introduction goes well or sideways. For Alison and others, the point of making introductions is to make things happen, not just to make introductions.

Failing to follow up is a networking screwup in another way too: you sabotage all your hard-networked ambitions when you lose your persistence to follow up. Early in his career, investor and entrepreneur Evan Nisselson really wanted a job as an associate photo editor. Beyond being an amateur photographer, Evan had no experience, so it was highly unlikely he could simply apply and land such a job. But Evan had persistence that led to an introduction to a great photo agent who was not hiring. "If you were hiring," Evan inquired, "what would that job be?" The agent happily answered in great detail.

Following the meeting, Evan sent a thank-you note (it was the nineties, after all) and after not hearing anything back, he called the agent and left a message. He called again a few weeks later, to follow up on the initial conversation. This went on for weeks. Finally, the way to follow up and get a response hit him: do the job the agent had described! Evan thought about ten global news stories, the photographers who should shoot those stories, and the magazines that might publish the stories. He sent the agent his idea, together with press clippings, in a big envelope.

Guess what? Still no response!

So, wondering if the envelope had been lost in the post, Evan called and left a message. Again there was no response. And two weeks later, he called again, but *this* time he spoke with the agent's assistant and got connected to the agent—who just happened to be in the office for the first time in months.

The end result? Evan started working as an associate photo editor the next morning. And the agent is a great mentor and friend to this day.

Evan's persistence may seem extreme, especially if you're the type who, reading his story, thinks, "I'd have given up on this job possibility by now!" On the other hand, for those looking to network their career future into exciting new possibilities, the value of persistence (and creative value-add persistence, at that) is a networking reality and a way to jump ahead of the competition and make powerful connections to land those dream opportunities.

Nothing to Say?—Good

One of my favorite YouTube videos was created by Pizza Hut.[40] Yes, Pizza Hut. It is not only a brilliant, well-written parody on the dangers of selfie sticks, but only at the end of the viral video do you realize that you've just watched a two-and-a-half-minute commercial for pizza delivery. It doesn't contain a sales pitch or two-for-one pizza delivery lures, nothing about the brand at all. By leaving itself out of the conversation, Pizza Hut draws us into one with them.

There's a lesson in that video: you can connect more effectively by saying less. Thinking about the endless promotions, events, and updates from big brands that clutter my e-mail inbox, a few suggestions come to mind:

- Stop pushing and start pulling! Draw me into a conversation with something delightful and surprising. If you haven't figured it out yet, it's *engagement* that drives connections and commerce.
- Include substantial content, not just the latest news. Inform me! Make me feel more in the know or more connected to you and your goals.
- Focus on community, not cold calls. I'm in awe of the skills of the door-to-door salesman—the steel ego that navigates the terrain of rejection. However, I turn to my community for insights, recommendations, and directions. If a post I've written somehow leads you to believe that I may like to try your product or service, that's an invitation to start building a relationship, not an invitation to pitch a monthly beauty box subscription to me.
- Remember that a good story has many chapters. Don't simply tell your customers or clients how great you are once and expect them to believe you. Show them over and over again, and engage them to tell your story and spread their appreciation of your greatness.

The Elevator Pitch

What is more anxiety causing: having to hear one more elevator pitch or having to craft your own? There is nothing more awkward than being introduced to someone (whether it is at a party or reception or event) and then immediately having to listen to the person's pitch, rather than starting a conversation. But you need to have your elevator pitch ready, because there is one un-expected place you really need to nail it: a Q&A session at a conference or event.

Picture this typical conference Q&A session scenario for a moment. You're at the Women Entrepreneurs Festival in New York City, and investor Joanne Wilson has just finished her key-note interview with Diane von Furstenberg. Joanne then opens up the remaining time for Q&A. You rush the microphone and . . . How do you maximize *the* moment when more than four hundred sets of conference-attendee eyes in a sold-out room are on you? With a well-crafted elevator pitch.

Most people blow the opportunity. They forget to say who they are. They don't really have a question and just want to share their "smarts." We've all sat through this. It is agonizing.

What you should do is say, "My name is X. I do Y," or "My startup solves X problem," or "I'm a student at Z. My question is, _____." Be quick, clear, and concise in connecting everyone in the room to who you are, what you do, and why they may just want to talk to you after the event. As for the in-sightful question you asked the speaker? It's the perfect conver-sation starter, now, isn't it?

Testing—One, Two, Three

Being responsive, courteous, and avoiding alienation are chal-lenges in the digital age. Sending and receiving e-mail often reminds me of the homeroom-attendance-taking scene in the classic movie *Ferris Bueller's Day Off*: "Bueller? . . . Bueller? . . . Bueller?"

Who doesn't feel like Bueller's high school economics teacher every time they send an e-mail? A response, any response, a nod, some tiny acknowledgment that we've been heard is all anyone is really looking for. So, in an informal world, even the e-mail autoresponse can relieve the anxiety of feeling ignored or overlooked.

Acknowledgment by autoresponse may be slightly below the bar of common courtesy in Miss Manners's book—it is not a "real" handwritten response, after all. However, it is prompt and, being practical, I think sometimes it's better than nothing. So is understanding. Understanding that lives are busy, Gmail messes up at times, and cats walk across computer keyboards deleting everything in their attention-seeking wake. When you feel your e-mail is being ignored, send it politely again. And follow up again after that too.

On the receiving end: when you discover a long-overlooked e-mail, acknowledge it. Your explanation doesn't need to be detailed—simply make it genuine and close the networking loop.

"I'm Your Biggest Fan"

Four words that devalue skill and knowledge by trying to disguise a networking need with flattery? "I'm your biggest fan."

On this subject Alison Levine, who has heard it all, offers some solid networking advice (which I've shared earlier in this book): "Do your homework before you approach people for a big ask. Find out what is important to them. If you cannot take the time to google someone and scour their website and their social media feeds to gather as much information as you can about them before approaching them for help, then they shouldn't waste their time helping you."

Skip the empty praise, because if that is the best reason you can come up with for someone to help you, you haven't thoroughly analyzed your need from the other person's perspective. When approached for help, busy, connected people (like Alison) want one thing: a genuine ask, backed up with a substantive reason why they should help you. You need to be able to answer this question: why should this person enthusiastically *want* to use their network of connections to help you?

Not Saying Thank You

In the book *Elements of Etiquette: A Guide to Table Manners in an Imperfect World*,[41] dining expert Craig Claiborne writes, on the subject of sending a note of thanks:

> The host of any dinner party deserves, at the very least, a phone call the next day. After more formal or special dinners, a thank-you note (on plain, but high-quality stationery) shows great consideration. A casual note or even a clever postcard will do nicely for more informal gatherings. In any event, a thank-you note should be received no more than one week after the dinner.

Of course, that was in 1992. Just as text messages have replaced phone calls (and grateful guests post #thanks on Instagram in lieu of sending a note), urgency and real time have replaced consideration in many of our daily interactions. In a mobile world, we're sending asks faster and less thoughtfully. To borrow from Evan Nisselson, "With mobile and social, the office is never closed and we're now in possession of more tools to ask for more."

Thankfully you can put a stop to these modern networking bad habits with these suggestions:

- Don't leave the host guessing about the RSVP list. Accept or decline invitations promptly. Then live up to your RSVP commitment (or at the very least change your response in a reasonable time before the actual event).
- If the event is a public one (e.g., a meetup, conference, or reception), publicly affirm with a tweet or post on Facebook or Instagram that you're planning to attend. Promoting an event you've been invited to is an excellent way to thank the host or event organizer.
- Ask the host if there is a hashtag for the event and if there are any special moments they want captured on social media—it's the digital way of asking "Is there anything I can do to assist you?"
- After the event, send a personalized thank-you note, whether digital or on paper (Red Stamp makes this very easy).

Your ability to network successfully—that is, your ability to build strong relationships—is based on trust and the quality of your connections, not on whether the number of your Twitter followers increased because of a trending hashtag. Relationships shape your professional road map, not fast Facebook friends. Inserting some good, old-fashioned, predigital consideration back into your networking exchanges will make you stand apart from the crowd.

8

Test, Fail, Learn, and Scale

You've made it—a few more pages then off you go, energized to make better use of the networking tools at your disposal, to more powerfully build the relationships you need. Your challenge once you put down this book is to transform old rules into new networking opportunities.

New networking glitters with open, unlimited access but needs to be infused with classic rules of etiquette. Check your spelling and put your feet in the shoes of your intended connection before you hit Send, Tweet, Post, or Snap.

New networking doesn't ask permission, so you shouldn't either! Do you need to wait till you have acquired all the skills required for your dream job to start networking within that profession? Absolutely not!

New networking is peer driven and highly participatory, just like the sharing economy. Forging strong bonds with your peers is as necessary, and valuable, as connecting with "higher-ups."

Have the ways we build relationships really changed that much? Yes—but in many ways, also not so much. Friends share on Facebook, and so do corporate colleagues on socially astute internal collaboration platforms. Traditional power structures still exist (think elite networking opportunities like TED) but now sit alongside democratized, highly accessible idea platforms (like TEDx). Ideas don't spread very far (and new opportunities won't be uncovered) if you're not open to new ways of providing access.

Don't Hit Pause

An e-mail from a friend, late one Saturday evening, reminded me of the classic Heinz Ketchup ad from 1979[42]—waiting in high expectation and anticipation for something really good to land on our plates. The friend was in the middle of interviewing for a new job. His initial meetings and exchanges with the potential employer were enthusiastic, energetic, and fast paced. The reasonable expectation of this seasoned, experienced professional was that he would land the job in a few weeks, so he should start planning the transition! All his other business conversations, informational interviews, and network expanding efforts were put way on the back burner.

I, the optimistic realist, wasn't particularly surprised by his e-mail:

> *I am still on hold with this firm. The managing partner says they have gotten sidetracked in trying to decide whether to have the [role] responsible for [another function] as well. Does it take two months to figure this out? It is time for me to move forward . . .*

Move forward? Reality check, my friend: you shouldn't have paused your networking activities in the first place! Adjust or ease up a little, maybe, but never stop. My friend's decision to wait and to continue waiting and waiting for a particular opportunity moved him back more than several networking paces. Two months later, he was back at networking stage one all over again, awkwardly trying to figure out how to reignite stale conversations and source new employment opportunities.

The rather obvious moral of this networking story: don't wait, don't check out, don't anticipate a result or response, and never hit Pause on the relationship-building machine. Anticipation of an expected result clouds your judgment, dulls your edge, and shifts your focus. Don't ever halt your networking efforts, even if you have a better than average expectation of an immediate job offer.

You Will Drop the Networking Ball

You will make networking mistakes, like saying the wrong thing at the company holiday party or not giving enough care to your social media platforms. And guess what? That's okay. Describing Twitter, I once remarked, "It's like a cocktail party: you'll meet some good people; you'll have spirited debates, learn some new things, and have a few awkward exchanges too; and, yes, you'll spill wine every once in a while, just as you do IRL."

Don't fret about your mistakes. Just don't make them regular bad habits—you don't want to be known as "that" person at the party. Move beyond them by learning from the experience and renewing your networking activities with a determined, considerate focus. And apologize while you mop up the wine you spilled.

Build to Last

When I was interviewing House of Genius's Jonathan Beninson, he said to me as he reflected on how he networks now: "You're gonna spend time with people, people you'll trust with your success and failures, so find people you want to spend time with."

Networking has always been and will always be about people. I can't say this enough, and Jonathan—as well as Kathryn, Alison, Erin, Evan, Aidan, and Tina—will back me up on this! This is classic networking etiquette and doesn't require an upgrade along with a new mobile app—it needs to be the underlying feature of whatever mobile device or platform or venue you're using to build relationships. You're going to need to call upon your relationships in a multitude of ongoing ways as you pursue your ambitions and design, not just for your career but in building the life you want to lead.

The truth is, you don't need to know that many people to have an intensely powerful network. You just need to know how to ask the right questions to purposefully connect to those relationships you have.

Assess, Reuse, and Recycle

It's not the load that breaks you down, it's the way you carry it.

—Lou Holtz

My guess is that you may still have some lingering doubts about whether you have enough time and energy in a 24-7 world for all this networking activity. And the answer is: Yes. You. Do. And after reading this book, you have the insights you need into how to be smarter about all the swiping/posting/chatting/growing that you are already doing day in and day out!

Building relationships, however, is not as seamless as the onboarding process for new users of an online marketplace. There is no shortcut to hack strong relationships! The work around? Make sure all your networking activities are working for you by aiming all (and I mean *all*) your networking actions toward your goal. Synchronizing your IRL handshake with your digital one is a worthwhile effort and the best use of your networking time.

Needs and Networks Evolve

Personal commitment doesn't mean much if you can't contribute to a meeting, make some outreach calls, attend a breakfast networking session—you know, do the minimal viable amount required. And, yes, the minimal amount is more than simply dialing it in, going through the motions by showing up once in a while. Commitment in name only is simply a word on a page (like an RSVP for an event you thought you might attend unless something better comes along).

Time is a double-edged sword. Investing my time in various networks, organizations, causes, and groups has been incredible career fuel! How else do I explain where I am today? I realize, however, I wasn't simply a member of a group or benefit committee or listserv, I was an active participant—or I resigned, freeing up time to invest my time in something else (in fact, during the course of finishing the first draft of this book, I resigned from two startup accelerator boards, realizing I no longer had the bandwidth or day-to-day ecosystem insights to contribute meaningfully to the organizations).

Pull out your weekly to-do list or monthly planner and review how you're spending your time. Are your volunteer or committee obligations still aligned with your goals? If not, it may be time to declutter some of those commitments.

Be a Lifelong Learner

In my 2015 commencement address at Marymount School of New York, I said to the graduating class:

> Curiosity and inquiry are the only skills that will not
> be obsolete in five years.

And while I started writing this book with more than a few opinions, I also tested my "networking know-how" and "superconnector status" by turning to my network for the case studies that have appeared throughout it. Remaining curious and open to change has its benefits. Here are some reminders of the most valuable insights I have gathered during this process, which I hope have now been passed on to you for your own future benefit:

Introverts are great networkers. It came as an intriguing surprise to realize that the people behind so many of the successful networking stories in this book classified themselves as introverts. Perhaps they are so successful precisely because they are more deliberate in taking control of their networking actions (a way to manage the discomfort of "going outside your comfort zone," perhaps?). "Network like an introvert" may become my go-to networking advice!

You need networks to see a bigger picture of who you are and what your opportunities can be. When Tina Roth Eisenberg dropped this revelation during our interview, a wave of relief hit me: I'm not the only one who has needed the mirror of a network to see a better picture of myself! You shouldn't be your only career confidant. While self-assessments have tremendous value, a 360-review (or seeking advice from a mentor or colleague) may reveal the bigger talents you should be unleashing. Separate your ambitions from inner self-chatter and test them out on your network.

Figure out what you are passionate about, as that passion fuels your networking stamina. For Aidan Donnelley Rowley, it is a love of books. For me, it is seeing others succeed that lifts my networking energy level.

Accept what you can control when you are building relationships and manage what you cannot. Time is out of your hands; focusing your efforts is not. Think about Joe Styler's unwavering focus on learning the skills for a job that he hadn't been offered, or Devon Brooks's four-year journey to a board seat.

Stick to networking basics—without regard to platform. I was moderately amused when I realized digital native Joe Styler's career-networking approach traced a route that sounded awfully like Janet Hanson's circa 1977 internal-advancement story. Platforms like LinkedIn haven't disrupted networking basics; they have simply provided more transparent networking tools for you to meaningfully execute your career plan.

Be amphibious in your approach to networking. It's not a question of IRL or digital. It's both. You need to move seamlessly between networking rooms, recognizing that your most meaningful, connected communications may happen in person and simultaneously on Viber, Gchat, WhatsApp, Kik, Snapchat, or the next communication platform or tool of choice.

Remember to ask why. Before you find yourself stuck in a stale conversation or wondering why you succumbed to FOMO, take the time to consider how any new effort is going to advance your goals. Your time (together with your relationships) is your most valuable asset—so ensure the time you spend attending, liking, or posting adds up to results.

Improvise and problem solve. In 2013, British Airways invited a hundred "forward-thinking founders, CEOs, venture capitalists, and Silicon Valley game-changers"[43] to board a flight from San Francisco to London and hack the global misalignment of tech talent in midair—a tech hackathon at thirty-thousand feet, with no Wi-Fi and a hundred type A personalities. Thanks to Mashable, I found myself on that flight too[44] (hacking a solution to the women in tech problem alongside a talented, rogue team of innovators who gathered the night before the flight in a hotel bar). Hackathons (intense time- and resource-constrained problem-solving exercises) provide a valuable networking lesson: sometimes you have to improvise. You're unlikely to ever find yourself in a scenario where time, resources, and contacts perfectly align. Embrace the creative challenge of constraint—rather than always holding it up, over and over again, as an excuse.

And in case you're wondering: first-class airline seats are not designed for collaboration.

Three More Ps

I know. I said the three Ps of networking are people, people, people. However, there are three more you need to keep in mind: persistence, planning, and politeness.

Your network won't build itself and won't happen overnight—even with a Facebook plug-in. Don't get discouraged. Keep at it! A swipe may get you a date, but building real relationships is a lifelong investment in other people.

Don't place your career bets on karma or help-wanted ads. Today's networkers use every available tool at their disposal to inform their research and to figure out where they fit within the bigger picture. They find and leverage connections. This is how you magically get out in front of opportunities.

It's a people-driven economy, and tech is a wonderful enabler of the communication process. The proliferation of apps, platforms, and tech tools is just more evidence of an ongoing need to connect—with courtesy and more than a little considerate attention—in order to have our ideas affirmed and requests for help acknowledged.

Stop Committing Random Acts of Networking

Whether you are working for a company or transitioning to a new career or launching your own venture, realize you're the entrepreneur of your career. Continuous learning, developing new skills, and actively seeking unique opportunities to advance personal and professional fulfillment are the new work/life normal—as is the ability to effectively connect with the people who can help you. Recognize that your next great opportunity may arrive at any time, from anyone, located anywhere. No more doubts, guessing, or hesitating about how to start networking your dreams. You now have a road map to strategically put yourself in front of the opportunities you're seeking and network your ambitions.

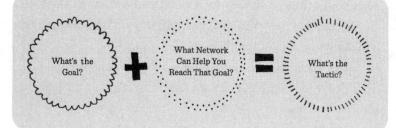

And let's stay connected. Drop by jkellyhoey.co for additional tips and tools. Jump into the conversations with me on Twitter @jkhoey. Add your voice to my posts on LinkedIn. And share your networked career stories at #BuildYourDreamNetwork and #BYDN.

Acknowledgments

To MY NETWORK for enthusiastically encouraging me to write this book—thank you. And h/t to Timm Whitney for admonishing me to "tell people what I do."

To Katie Workman, Elmira Bayrasli, and Liza Kindred, who guided me at the proposal stage. Words cannot express my enormous gratitude for your advice.

Special thanks to Jonathan Beninson, Evan Nisselson, Erin Newkirk, Joe Styler, Sandy Cross, Jennifer Johnson Scalzi, Manisha Thakor, Rachel Hofstetter, Lois Herzeca, Varelie Croes, Tina Roth Eisenberg, Jessica Peltz-Zatulove, Claudia Batten, Kathryn Finney, Alison Levine, Janet Hanson, Aidan Donnelley Rowley, Devon Brooks, the JumpFund's Tiffanie Robinson and Shelley Prevost, Rob Hayes, Elena Rossini, Andrew Grill, and Amanda Ellis for generously sharing your networking stories. This book would not have come together without your expert insights.

I owe many thanks to my designer, the enormously talented Gena Cuba, who brilliantly translated my words into visual explanations, and to Elizabeth Talerman for introducing me to Gena.

To my literary agent, Brandi Bowles, a massive thank-you for taking that first meeting and believing in my vision. And to my editor Jeanette Shaw, thank you for challenging me with your deadlines! To my editor Stephanie Bowen, thank you for so enthusiastically guiding my book to completion. This goal-focused former attorney could not have asked for more perfect editors to work with.

I also want to thank all my friends, followers, and connections for years of RTs, likes, shares, regrams, and posts. To my newsletter subscribers (especially Alain Bankier, who swears he reads it every week), your feedback has fueled my writing and guided me to find my voice.

This book was nurtured at its start—and its finish—on Saint Kitts. So to Maurice, Janaki, Georgia, Grace, Maeve, Kaye, Nile, and the rest of my Saint Kitts family, my heartfelt thanks for your encouragement and endless support.

Notes

1. Vanessa Van Edwards, "Are You an Ambivert?" *Science of People*: http://www.scienceofpeople.com/2014/12/ambivert-extrovert -introvert/.
2. Sara Horowitz and Fabio Rosati, "Freelancing in America: A National Survey of the New Workforce," Freelancersunion.org (September 2014): https://www.freelancersunion.org/blog/ dispatches/2014/09/04/53million/.
3. "The Sharing Economy—Sizing the Revenue Opportunity," PricewaterhouseCoopers: http://www.pwc.co.uk/issues/megatrends/ collisions/sharingeconomy/the-sharing-economy-sizing-the-revenue -opportunity.html.
4. "NASA Glenn Research Center Joins Cleveland Clinic's Global Healthcare Innovations Alliance," Cleveland Clinic (March 11, 2015): http://my.clevelandclinic.org/about-cleveland-clinic/ newsroom/releases-videos-newsletters/2015-3-11-nasa-glenn -research-center-joins-cleveland-clinics-global-healthcare -innovations-alliance.
5. Lisa Richwine, "Cox Developing Digital Home Health Services with Cleveland Clinic," Reuters (February 19, 2015): http://www.reuters .com/article/us-cox-comm-health-idUSKBN0LN07J20150219.
6. Eric Newcomer, "GM Invests $500 Million in Lyft," Bloomberg.com (January 4, 2016): http://www.bloomberg.com/news/articles/2016 -01-04/gm-invests-500-million-in-lyft-to-bolster-alliance-against-uber.

7. "The Agile Workplace: Supporting People and Their Work," Academia.edu (December 2001): https://www.academia.edu/ 2518397/THE_AGILE_WORKPLACE_SUPPORTING _PEOPLE_AND_THEIR_WORK_A_Research_Partnership _Between_Gartner_MIT_and_22_Industry_Sponsors.

8. Stefano Pogliani and Willem Gabilly, "IBM Social Computing Guidelines" (November 29, 2011): http://www.slideshare.net/ stefanopog/ibm-social-computing-guidelines.

9. "Benching: An Idea Whose Time Has Come . . . Again," Steelcase White Papers: http://www.steelcase.com/insights/white-papers/ benching-idea-whose-time-come/.

10. "Humantech, Inc.," Steelcase Case Studies (2013): http://www .steelcase.com/insights/case-studies/humantech-inc/.

11. Morten T. Hansen and Scott Tapp, "Who Should Be Your Chief Collaboration Officer?" *Harvard Business Review* (October 11, 2010): https://hbr.org/2010/10/who-should-be-your-chief-colla.

12. Brian Uzzi and Shannon Dunlap, "How to Build Your Network," *Harvard Business Review* (December 2005): https://hbr.org/2005/12/ how-to-build-your-network.

13. Rachel Hofstetter, *Cooking Up a Business* (New York: Perigee Books, 2013).

14. Claire Cain Miller, "Out of the Loop in Silicon Valley," *The New York Times* (April 17, 2010): http://www.nytimes.com/2010/04/18/ technology/18women.html?_r=0.

15. Gina Kolata, "Sharing of Data Leads to Progress on Alzheimer's," *The New York Times* (August 12, 2010): http://www.nytimes.com/2010/ 08/13/health/research/13alzheimer.html?pagewanted=all&_r=0.

16. "2015CF-The Crowdfunding Industry Report": http://www .crowdsourcing.org/editorial/global-crowdfunding-market-to-reach -344b-in-2015-predicts-massolutions-2015cf-industry-report/45376.

17. Kickstarter public stats page, updated daily: https://www.kickstarter .com/help/stats.

18. Alison Levine, *On the Edge: Leadership Lessons from Mount Everest and Other Extreme Environments* (New York: Grand Central Publishing, 2014).

19. Aidan Donnelley Rowley, *Life After Yes* (New York: HarperCollins / Avon, 2010).

20. Information on Happier Hours, including past guest authors, can be found at http://www.happierhours.com/.

21. Harriet Ruff, "Fortune 500 Under 40 @ IBM Astor Place NYC," harrietruff.com (November 5, 2015): http://harrietruff.com/ fortune-500-under-40-ibm-astor-place-nyc/ and Twitter https:// twitter.com/hashtag/500under40.

22. Nicole Torres, "Research: Technology Is Only Making Social Skills More Important," *Harvard Business Review* (August 15, 2015): https://hbr.org/2015/08/research-technology-is-only-making-social -skills-more-important.

23. Tom Rath and Jim Harter, PhD, "Your Friends and Your Social Wellbeing," *Gallup Business Journal* (August 19, 2010): http://www .gallup.com/businessjournal/127043/friends-social-wellbeing.aspx.

24. Steelcase, "Six Dimensions of Wellbeing in the Workplace," *360 Magazine* (67): http://www.steelcase.com/insights/articles/six -dimensions-of-wellbeing-in-the-workplace/.

25. *First Round Review* is found online at http://firstround.com/review/.

26. "English Coffeehouses, Penny Universities," Historic UK: http:// www.historic-uk.com/CultureUK/English-Coffeehouses-Penny -Universities/.

27. Elena's documentary *Stargazer Lottie Doll in Space* can be viewed on YouTube: https://www.youtube.com/watch?v=_3I0ChExz-w.

28. "Social Media Usage: 2005–2015," Pew Research Center Report (October 8, 2015): http://www.pewinternet.org/2015/10/08/ social-networking-usage-2005-2015/.

29. Andrew Grill, "The Future of Social for Travel & How Millennials Are Shaking up the Industry," *Social Business Thinking*: http:// londoncalling.co/2015/10/the-future-of-social-for-travel-how -millennials-are-shaking-up-the-industry/.

30. Stefano Pogliani and Willem Gabilly, "IBM Social Computing Guidelines."

31. Aaron Smith, "Searching for Work in the Digital Era," Pew Research Center Report (November 19, 2015): http://www .pewinternet.org/2015/11/19/searching-for-work-in-the-digital-era/.

32. Harriet Ruff's travel- and food-loving alter ego is found on Twitter @ hattyruff and on Facebook: https://www.facebook.com/thesunniersideup/ timeline.

33. Novelist Aidan Donnelley Rowley can be found on Instagram at @adonnrowley. Happier Hours is the literary salon Aidan founded in 2010 before publishing her first book, *Life After Yes*: http://www .happierhours.com/.

34. Andrew Grill, "The Future of Social."

35. Malcolm Gladwell, *The Tipping Point: How Little Things Can Make a Big Difference* (Boston: Little Brown, 2000).

36. *The New York Times* maintains a public list of all its journalists on Twitter: https://twitter.com/nytimes/lists/nyt-journalists?lang=en. So does *The Washington Post*: http://www.washingtonpost.com/wp-dyn/content/linkset/2008/09/16/LI2008091601031.html. Most other media outlets maintain similar lists.

37. Gillian Morris, "How We Got to 200,000 Users with No Marketing Spend," Gillian Morris (blog): http://gillian.im/2014/12/200k-users-no-marketing-spend.html.

38. Vivek Wadhwa, "The Glaring Gender Dilemma Silicon Valley Venture Capitalists Are Hiding From," *The Washington Post* (October 7, 2014): https://www.washingtonpost.com/news/innovations/wp/2014/10/07/the-glaring-gender-dilemma-silicon-valley-venture-capitalists-are-hiding-from/.

39. Chris Fralic, "The Art of the Email Introduction: 10 Rules for Emailing Busy People," *Forbes* (March 27, 2013): http://www.forbes.com/sites/bruceupbin/2013/03/27/the-art-of-the-email-introduction-10-rules-for-emailing-busy-people/.

40. *The Dangers of Selfie Sticks PSA*, Pizza Hut: https://www.youtube.com/watch?v=1fmQs37YqXg.

41. Craig Claiborne, *Elements of Etiquette: A Guide to Table Manners in an Imperfect World* (New York: William Morrow, 1992).

42. If you weren't around when the ad originally aired on TV, you can watch it on YouTube: https://youtu.be/uoLoyg3JKRQ.

43. Details on the British Airways "UnGrounded" innovation initiative can be founded at http://ungroundedthinking.com/tagged/theFlight.

44. "Industry Pioneers to Join British Airways Aboard 'UnGrounded' Innovation Lab Held at 30,000 Feet," *Businesswire* (May 22, 2013): http://www.businesswire.com/news/home/20130522005943/en/Industry-Pioneers-Join-British-Airways-Aboard-%E2%80%98UnGrounded%E2%80%99.

ABOUT THE AUTHOR

Most information about J. Kelly Hoey can be found online—and is posted by her.

As a connector and networking expert, Kelly has been lauded in venues from *Forbes* ("one of five women changing the world of VC/entrepreneurship") to *Fast Company* ("25 Smartest Women on Twitter"). Creating and sharing content is just one of the many ways she stays connected to her vast network of diverse relationships. In addition to tweeting frequently @jkhoey and writing a weekly newsletter, Kelly has a column on Inc.com, interviews intriguing founders in her network for myturnstone .com, and maintains a blog on jkellyhoey.co (as well as on Medium).

She's practiced law in Toronto; spoken to audiences around the world, from Beirut to Aruba to Auckland; interviewed leading Silicon Valley investors; and dined with Malala. No, Kelly never envisioned a career filled with so many twists and turns (and tweets).

When she's not online or on a plane, Kelly resides in New York City.

As for that *J* in J. Kelly Hoey, for some reason her parents decided to call their middle child by her middle name.